MORE MOD BUILDINGS

IN 4MM AND 7MM

GEOFF TAYLOR

GT BUILDINGS (GEOFF TAYLOR) PUBLISHING

Copyright GT Buildings (Geoff Taylor) Publishing 2012
ISBN 978-0-9572827-0-4

Designed by Geoff Taylor

Published by
GT BUILDINGS (GEOFF TAYLOR) PUBLISHING
2 Wern Cottages, Bwlch-y-ffridd, Newtown, Powys, SY16 3HX

Printed by Creative Digital Printing Limited, Shrewsbury

CONTENTS

INTRODUCTION 1

LAYOUT FOCUS -
   DEWSBURY MIDLAND 2
   CONSTRUCTION OF DEWSBURY MIDLAND 8

EASTLEIGH WATER TOWER 12

SUTTON PARK STATION 14

LAYOUT FOCUS -
   THE GRESLEY BEAT 16
   CONSTRUCTION OF THE GRESLEY BEAT 22

ASHBOURNE ENGINE SHED 28

LLANDUDNO STATION 29

KILMACOLM STATION 30

CANAL WHARF 33

LAYOUT FOCUS -
   BURNDEN PARK 34
   CONSTRUCTION OF BURNDEN PARK 40
   CONSTRUCTION OF NEW BURNDEN PARK 43

TERRACE, GOODS SHED AND WATER TOWER ... 46

HOTEL AND FOOTBRIDGE 47

LAYOUT FOCUS -
   MILTON HALL 48
   CONSTRUCTION OF MILTON HALL 56

BRIDGE FOR BUCKFASTLEIGH 64

PLATFORMS FOR BUCKFASTLEIGH 65

LAYOUT FOCUS -
   EDGWARE ROAD UNDER CONSTRUCTION 66

BRICK TERRACES WITH PUB 70

THREE BRIDGES ENGINE SHED 72

LAYOUT FOCUS -
   WHITECHAPEL UNDER CONSTRUCTION......... 76

FOUNTAIN HOTEL 84

TREES AND WALLS 87

ST. MARY'S CHURCH 88

SUMMIT TUNNEL 93

LOUTH STATION 94

LAYOUT FOCUS -
   BARMOUTH JUNCTION 96
   CONSTRUCTION OF BARMOUTH JUNCTION 102

BRICK TERRACE ON HILL............................... 108

LIGHTING IN BUILDINGS................................ 111

STONE TERRACE WITH END HOUSE................ 112

BRIDGE FOR APPLEBY.................................... 114

INFORMATION 116

Appleby station

INTRODUCTION

I make model buildings to commission and work in both 4mm and 7mm scales, constructing a vast selection of different buildings for railway and town areas. Many of them have been fixed on exhibition layouts, but there have also been many more on private layouts, which most people will not get a chance to look at.

In this book I describe, with construction details and pictures, how I make some of these models. All photographs have been taken by myself, except where indicated.

The most well known layouts that I have worked on to date are Dewsbury Midland and The Gresley Beat, both of which are large 4mm scale exhibition layouts. These two very popular layouts can be seen all over the country at exhibitions and both have been a very good way of showing my models off to the general public over the last few years.

At some of the exhibitions, I demonstrate how to create my models and try to answer all the questions that are asked.

My first book; Creating Model Buildings in 4mm and 7mm, has a great deal of my building techniques shown, with one model being constructed in its entirety from scratch.

I have also made a DVD about my models, called Building Buildings, which is in the Right Track series.

Various articles have been printed in Model Railway Journal, British Railway Modelling and Railway Modeller.

Over the years, many modellers have asked me about plans for cottages and houses etc., so in this book, I've included some to help in the construction of the models. Of course, you don't have to make the ones that I have included here, but you could change them around, make them larger, add different details to them, or even just look at the dimensions of windows and doors to get a feel of what you want to achieve.

By far the best way forward, is to find a building you want to model and measure it yourself and then, after making it, you should have found that very satisfying.

I wish to thank the owners of the layouts and buildings for giving me a chance to build some great and interesting models for them.

I hope this book inspires you to make some really good models.

Geoff Taylor

LAYOUT FOCUS -
DEWSBURY MIDLAND

4mm scale
British Railways period

I am part of the Manchester Model Railway Society team, who have constructed this layout. It has been displayed at exhibitions in different parts of the country.

Although the layout doesn't portray an actual real station, it is based on what could have been if the Midland Railway had built its proposed line from Royston, on the Sheffield to Leeds line, to Bradford via

The large mill towers above everything in the town.

My first model for the Dewsbury Midland layout was this terrace on a slope. It looked so much better when it was bedded in. I carved all the setts for the road individually from DAS modelling clay, but later on made a four sett mould tool, which made life a lot easier.

This view, looking up the road to the chapel, can be seen from inside the layout.

Dewsbury. Many of the models in the town scene are based on real ones in Dewsbury and a few have been chosen from further afield.

Dewsbury Midland has many features that you would see in the West Yorkshire area, especially in the town of Dewsbury. A few field trips were made around the chosen area of Dewsbury and the surrounding countryside. Many photographs were taken of buildings that would look good on the layout and in the end, there were far too many, so we had to decide on the

Different levels of steps are quite a feature around this area and add character to the scene.

The models and backscene blend perfectly. A few different modellers have made these houses, but they all look the part together.

The houses next to the chapel and, below, a close-up of one of them.

ones that would fit in with the design of the layout. On the model, the landscape, roads and buildings have all been designed to look the part and compliment each other, so that the viewer will know which area it has been set in.

As far as the buildings were concerned, many months were spent moving cardboard mock-ups around until we were satisfied with the result. Different views through alleyways, backyards and up hills, were carefully thought out, which would give the viewer a good idea of what the area modelled was all about.

At first, some of the buildings had extended bases on them, which would sit on the baseboard, but it soon became apparent that it was better to make them with only a few cms of extra base. The models could then be placed higher or lower where the landscape dictated their position. Even at the last moment, some

More Model Buildings - Dewsbury Midland 5

A nice view looking under the viaduct arches. The water was made by painting the base and glueing stones and gravel onto it, before countless layers of varnish were applied.

6 Dewsbury Midland - *More Model Buildings*

The front of this terrace is usually hard to see for the general public, but it shows that all details have been done properly. The steps at the back were constructed fully at the bottom and then gradually getting to low relief going into the backscene.

All yards have outside toilets and could do with some clutter to soften the scene.

buildings were slightly re-arranged in position to get the best possible effect.

Being very much an urban setting with many buildings, the construction of the buildings took a very long time and so a few more modellers helped out and some were shown how to make them. This is where joining a model railway club really benefits the modeller. All manner of skills can be acquired in different aspects of the hobby.

Even after all this time, there are still a few details to be added to try and make it look even better. For a long-term project like Dewsbury, you can take time to get things right and that is one of the reasons why the layout is very popular at exhibitions.

**Check out the exhibition calendars for dates that Dewsbury Midland is being exhibited.
Also, the home page on my website has details of what shows it is going to attend.**

Articles on the layout have appeared in Railway Modeller, British Railway Modelling, Hornby Magazine, Model Rail and Model Railway Journal.

More Model Buildings - Dewsbury Midland 7

Left is the entrance to the Bank in the High Street, seen in the picture to the right, but unfortunately this view can't be seen at exhibitions.

The mill, which is modelled in low-relief, straddles both a road and a stream, so it makes an interesting building to model. The real building is situated near the Worth Valley Railway in Yorkshire.

CONSTRUCTION OF DEWSBURY MIDLAND LAYOUT

It took approximately ten years to get the layout into a more or less exhibitable state and it has been worked on, little by little, ever since. We had static signals on the layout for some time, but they have gradually been changed to working ones, which has made it a lot more interesting to view and to operate.

A small group of us constructed the buildings and scenics, while others made the trackwork and the woodwork, such as the baseboards and supporting beams and legs. The engines, coaches and wagons are owned and maintained by individual members and I have to say that they run marvellously most of the time, considering how many times they travel

The viaduct end of the layout. We must have been satisfied with this area, as it looks very similar now on the finished layout. Note the viaducts are being clad in stonework. These are various resin castings from masters, made by Martin Stringer and a very good job it was as well.

Mock-ups are a very important aspect of making a layout. The card buildings can be moved around until the scenes look right. These first two photos were the very basis of the finished scenes.

A very early photo of the steep hill end of the layout. As you can see, lots of cardboard buildings and roads are being moved around to get a good effect. Little did we know at this time, that a moving road vehicle system would be put in, after we had built the scene!

round the layout at each exhibition.

Although the majority of the buildings have been modelled from real ones, over a wide area of West Yorkshire, the actual streets don't exist. Instead, we have endeavoured to capture the atmosphere of the area with different levels and so have positioned buildings on hills and obscured some slightly, so that viewers have to peer round them in order to see the details. Of course, the viaducts do that same thing splendidly and different views can be had by peering under each of the arches.

Mostly, the general public see Dewsbury Midland at exhibitions and as such, have no idea how we managed to make the whole layout happen, so here are some photographs of it during construction.

Before any models were started, rough card mock-ups were created with card roads. Everything was balanced on bits of wood to get the desired effect. This process took many months to get right and by changing the angles and heights, we eventually got to a position which we could then go ahead with and so the lengthy job of creating the models could really begin.

I would like to give a big thanks to the Manchester Model Railway Society for really starting me on the road (tracks?) to making models for a living.

The mill, which has both road and stream going through it, and the adjacent warehouse. Note the white plastic bases, which for these models gives the correct height from baseboard. This is not always the best method, as they cannot be lowered if needed. The warehouse to the right is a good example. The base could have been made a lot less deep, making it easier to position the height.

Compare these pictures with the ones of the finished layout in the previous pages. You can now see how we achieved the result. Various members of the Manchester Model Railway Society have made the models, scenery, baseboards and trackwork that can be seen in these construction pictures.

The viaduct end again, showing the large mill and at the back, a mock-up that didn't get into the finished layout. Many photo's were taken in and around the area, but not every building was modelled.

10 Construction of Dewsbury Midland - *More Model Buildings*

Look how different the viaduct scene was before the groundwork was started. Note also the viaduct piers before some of the stone cladding was applied and the rather unnecesssary deep plastic bases to the first batch of buildings. The hill was made by glueing polystyrene blocks together and carving them to get the contours. A thick coating of plaster was applied over the top and, where necessary, was carved into rocks.

More Model Buildings - Construction of Dewsbury Midland 11

Compare this picture with the one on page 10. This is the finished rock face above the tunnel.

Most of the buildings are now in place and scenery has been started. Also, the backscene has been attached, which has made a tremendous difference to the overall appearance.

EASTLEIGH WATER TOWER
4mm

This must be one of the largest water towers I have seen, subsequently the model of it is huge. Just think about all those gallons of water in the tank above the mess rooms!

It is located at Eastleigh, near Southampton, on the main line railway route from London to Southampton.

To help in the construction of it, many pictures were sent to me, showing various different angles, which enabled me to make a reasonably accurate and interesting model.

The model is constructed from plastic, with additional items in etched-brass, such as windows, louvres, doors, lintels and water tank sides.

Panels for the water tank part of this model were made in etched-brass, from my own artwork that was drawn on the computer. The roof is made up of scale corrugated sheets and each one has been overlapped slightly, to define the joins better.

The top louvres have also been made as an etch in a framework. I've glued a black painted piece of plastic behind each one, which gives the impression of a gloomy interior.

Entrance to the mess rooms is by the long covered porch. This has greatly enhanced the model and given it character. Also, the small corrugated iron shed is a nice extra feature.

More Model Buildings - Eastleigh Water Tower 13

The main part of the building has been made and painted. The next step is to add the windows, doors and louvres, before making the roof. I've made a base so that everything can be glued in place on to it.

Both ends of the model are shown here. The entrance to the gent's can be seen on one side, as well as the main water tank pipe. On the other end, one of the louvres is shown and the detail on the water tank shows up the rivets.

The entrance to the mess rooms can be found at either end of the covered porch.

SUTTON PARK STATION
4mm

I don't often get much chance to model a dilapidated station building, but this commission came along and it ended up being a very interesting one to make.

The long, red-bricked single-storey building has gables and tall chimneys and an outside gents toilet. A passage leads through the building from the platform to the forecourt. There is also a flat-roofed building and a small brick shed, which has survived being knocked down, unlike the ones next to it.

There are a few slates and ridge tiles missing, as well as a bit of graffiti on the walls. Boarded up windows make a nice feature on the model as well. The right-hand end of the building was still being used as offices for someone, so the windows have their glazing intact.

The station was situated on the Walsall to Castle Bromwich line, near Birmingham.

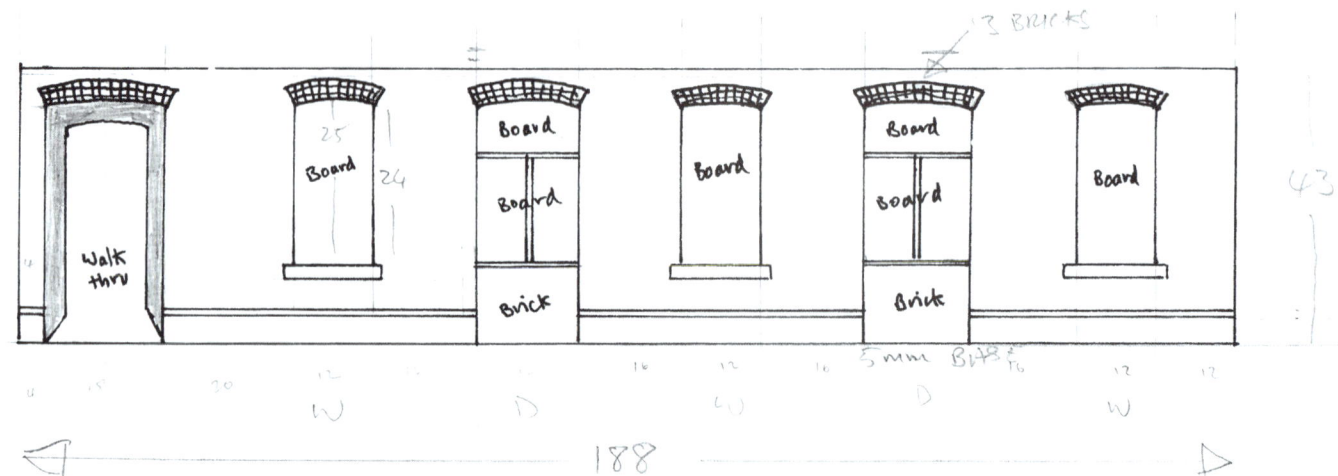

More Model Buildings - Sutton Park Station 15

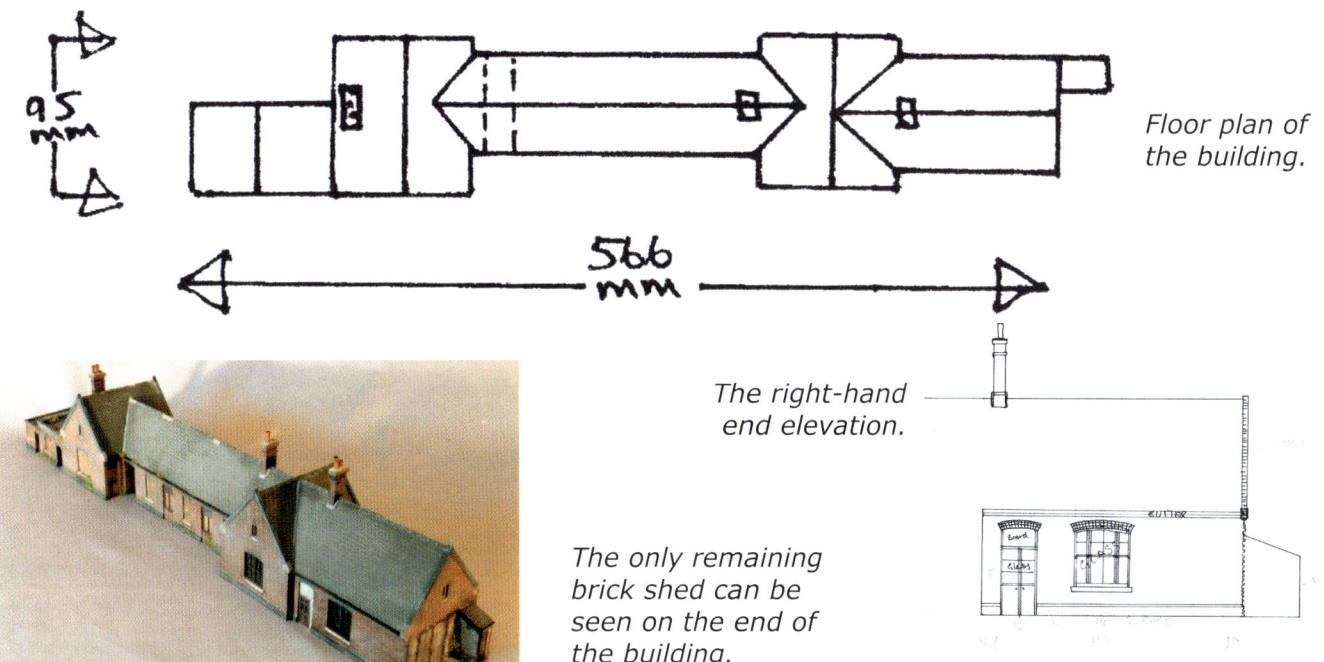

Floor plan of the building.

The right-hand end elevation.

The only remaining brick shed can be seen on the end of the building.

Above, the whole model and the picture below shows the gents toilet and flat roof building.

This shows the boarded up windows and doors. Note the partly-bricked up bases of the doorways.

LAYOUT FOCUS -
THE GRESLEY BEAT

4mm scale
LNER period, 1923 - 1939

This layout is privately owned, but is exhibited with the help of friends and I am priviledged to have been asked to be a regular operator on this very popular layout.

The Gresley Beat is a very large layout depicting the outskirts of King's Cross station in London. Although no station is modelled, you get the feeling that just through the tunnel, which is actually the entrance to the storage yard, the business of the station is quite hectic. Trains are arriving and departing on the main lines, while the goods lines are kept busy with the coal trains and other mixed goods.

The rolling stock is a mixture of kit-built and ready to run, with some beautiful rakes of coaches and many goods wagons and vans in long trains.

A real feature of the layout is the light engine workings, with many different loco's going back and forth from King's Cross station to the engine shed, turn on the turntable, get coaled and watered, or just put on shed.

The large engine shed,

The horse and cart for the coalman was made up from a kit and the signboard was designed on the computer and printed off. The railings are from my range of etches. The telephone boxes and lamp are also kits.

called 'Top Shed', plays a very important role on the layout and this is where I first came into the picture. This was my first commission for The Gresley Beat. As with most model railways, space on the layout was at a premium, so the engine shed was modelled smaller than the real one. Even so, it is still a large model and lots of details were added to make it as authentic as possible from the pictures that were given to me. The roof was made with a central lift-out section to enable 'lost loco's' to be retrieved.

After the engine shed, many other models were commissioned and most of the surrounding buildings for the shed area were then constructed, such as the water softening tower, signing on office, toilets, mess rooms and the coaling tower. The coaling tower had been made as a basic shell and I added everything else to it.

I was then asked to make a London scene of terraced houses, pub and funeral director's, complete with backyards, roads and pavements. All this was to be made on a sub-baseboard,

This is the water softening plant and the style of it would have been found in many of the engine shed areas, where water was of the hard type. The steps were made up individually from Evergreen strip and it was very difficult to get the right look on the curve and keep the treads level.

which would then be glued and screwed onto the main baseboard structure. I was given a few photographs of terraces and had more or less a free reign on how to achieve the end result. I have to say at this point, that I've not actually visited the area that I've modelled, so have been extremely pleased that so many viewers have remarked on how well it looks.

Some of the pictures on these Gresley Beat pages have been taken by Brian Longhurst, one of the operating team.

Above is the small mess rooms and stores building and below is part of the bridge for the North London line, with the goods sidings underneath.

More Model Buildings - The Gresley Beat 19

Top Shed area. A view taken from above the gasworks, showing the back end of the shed. The coaling plant is not a working model. The shell of it was made by Cliff Parsons to make sure it fitted the restricted space. I added all other details and painted it. Below is the toilet block.

20 The Gresley Beat - *More Model Buildings*

This is the view that the operators see from inside the layout.

This Gresley Beat feature would not be complete without pictures of the terraces and street scenes, so here a few of them, showing different aspects.

A coffin can be seen propped up in the shed, which belongs to the undertakers. Note also the ladder and cat on top of the roof.

More Model Buildings - The Gresley Beat 21

After all the hard work on making these models, it still gives me great pleasure seeing the layout again and looking down these streets.

CONSTRUCTION OF THE GRESLEY BEAT LAYOUT BUILDINGS

The main part of the layout, scenic-wise, is undoubtedly the street scene. The streets are on the front corner of the layout, which makes it easier for the public to see the buildings a lot closer at exhibitions.

Each terrace and building has been constructed on its own base. This enabled them to be glued in place, one by one, with the roads being built around them. They all have cellars, so the roads are actually raised from the baseboard to the correct height. This sort of construction could be useful on any layout, even without cellars to houses, as you could then build the road on a hill or incline.

These two photos show the make-up of the road and pavements. MDF and ply were used as bases and this gives a good sound base for adding the groundwork.

These are some of the outhouses for the terraces. Sometimes it is easier to make them up in batches, which means each part can be made at the same time.

The North London Railway line goes over this bridge and it is part of the structure that spans the whole width of the layout. The other part is the girder section, which spans the main lines to the left of this bridge.

One of the terraces, showing how the cellars and back yards have been constructed as a whole unit

The roads were made up from sheets of Wills setts. Each one has had the excess parts cut off and filed and sanded down. Any gaps were filled with Milliput. The pavements are the next part to make and that is plastic sheet that has been scribed into paving slabs.

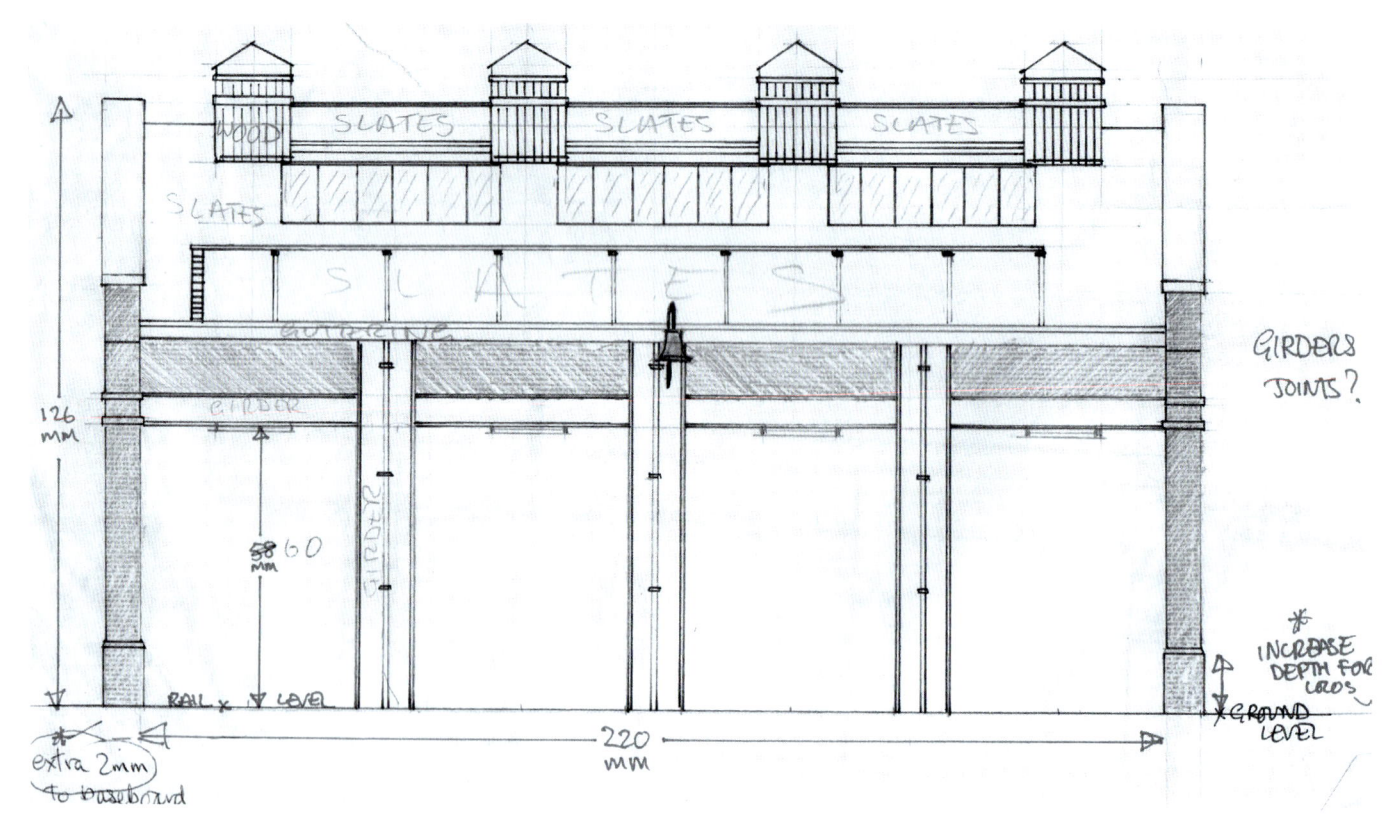

24 Construction of Top Shed - *More Model Buildings*

Fully detailed plans, drawn up to scale, showing the front elevation and part of one side of the Top Shed model. It is essential to get the measurements correct for a model like this for clearances of loco's.

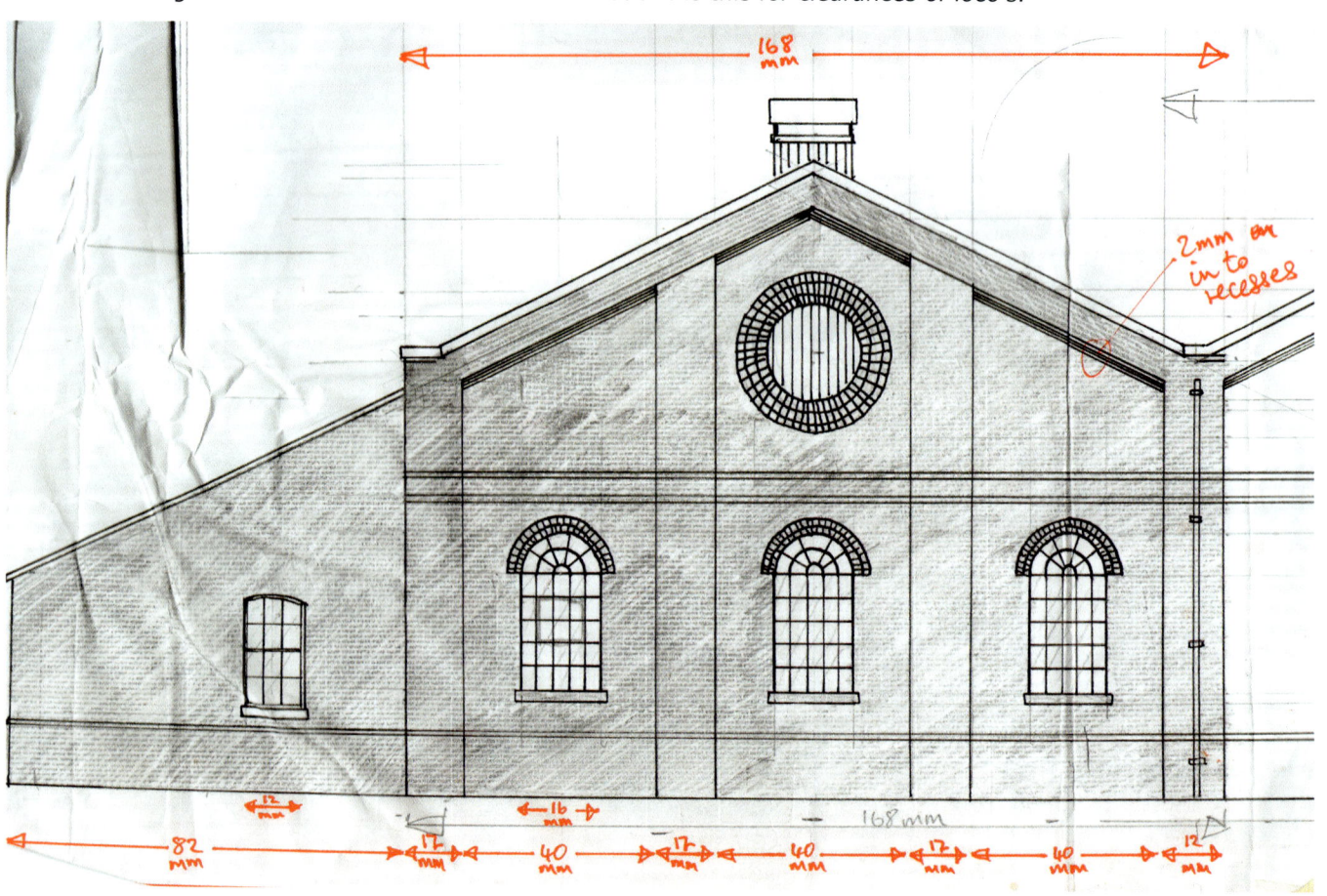

TOP SHED

As usual on most layouts, space was limited, so this model is only four tracks wide and not the eight, like the real one was. However, it has all the essentials and look of the real one. From photographs in books, lots of brick counting had to be done to get the dimensions for the model. This is not the easiest job to do, as the closer to the picture you get, the more out of focus it appears.

It is three feet (or 900mm) in length, so it is a very large model. It has a removable centre piece made up of three roofs, so that any loco that stalls inside can be retrieved.

The base material for the model was MDF, which would make it a lot stronger. As there were only five windows and five vents down each side, it meant that not too much cutting of the MDF was needed.

Walls have plinths and recesses, so a lot of working out of measurements was needed to enable me to get the size needed. The tracks through the shed had already been laid, so it was really essential to get this right.

The circular vents were quite a feature on the shed, so I made one master for the brick surrounds and prepared a mould to enable resin castings to be made. This ensured they all looked the same. The vent openers were scribed plastic and painted to resemble wood. I modelled some of them in the open position.

The twenty smoke vents were made with square timber bases covered in plastic sheet and then scored 20thou sheet was added for the wood planked doors.

For this model the skylights were made from clear acetate with plastic strips, cut to fit, but if I was making it again now I would use etched-brass frames.

The finished model, before being fixed on the layout. The clock was made with small pieces of plastic and the face drawn up on the computer

This was the first model that I constructed for The Gresley Beat layout.

At each end of the model, I glued a plank of wood on bearers that stretched the length of the model. This would enable the lift-out section to fit in the space between.

26 Construction of Top Shed - *More Model Buildings*

Aerial view of the shed from inside the layout.

Two of the small mess rooms.

The water softening plant was a bit tricky to make. The base is made up of twelve sides, which has a door and two different sizes of windows.

To get the cylinder shape of the holder, I used a thick cardboard tube and wrapped plastic sheet round it, A second layer of 20thou sheet was scored first to represent the plating, before being glued on. This top sheet was gently bent on the workbench to try to eliminate the plastic from springing out when fixed.

The access stairs to the top of the tower was quite a long and relatively hard job. Steps have been individually glued on to the side bearers in an attempt to get the model to look authentic.

MAIN OFFICE AT TOP SHED

Bricks have been added to the plastic shell and in the lower picture, the base colour has been painted.

The chimney stacks on my models have extra-long bases that are firmly attached to the walls of the buildings. This is a good example, showing the inside walls.

The finished model shows details such as the portico and small attached building with sliding doors. The weather vane has an etched brass Atlantic loco on top.

ASHBOURNE ENGINE SHED
4mm

This engine shed was located at Ashbourne in Derbyshire. The line ran from Buxton to Uttoxeter and was originally built by the LNWR.

The model is plastic construction using Slater's stone sheet, apart from the roof which is made from card with thin card slates. The window frames are etched-brass.

Doors have been made by scoring 40thou sheet plastic with a scriber and then adding plastic strip overlays for the framing. The main louvre vent and the smoke vents are made up from plastic strips.

Inside, the walls were painted white with a bit of grey and then a black wash was applied to get a rather dirty look.

LLANDUDNO STATION
4mm

These are pictures of an old layout, based on Llandudno Station in North Wales. It is probably the most completed layout that I had achieved at that time.

The station building, with canopy, was a reasonable model and constructed using photographs of the real thing, which was gradually being dismantled. I also used plans from a book on the station.

A mixture of LMS and GWR stock was used (just because I liked both!) and the layout ran to a six foot traverser. Quite a few wagon kits were made up with automatic un-coupling. I added a goods shed and yard next to the platforms. The turntable was scratch-built, using Meccano gears for the mechanism to turn it. All points were operated by wire in tube from levers at the baseboard edge.

The northlight engine shed was made using the drawings from the excellent book, LNWR Portrayed, by Jack Nelson. The signal box was modelled on the real one, which was still located at the plaftorm ends of Llandudno Station.

The home-made turntable.

KILMACOLM STATION
7mm

This station was to be found on the former Glasgow and South Western Railway line from Glasgow St. Enoch to Greenock Princess Pier, about 17 miles from Glasgow.

The model was constructed using an MDF base with DAS modelling clay attached and then carved into stones. The window stone surrounds were made up in plastic as a master, before making a rubber mould of it. Resin castings could then be produced, ensuring they were all identical. The door surrounds were all made from plastic and scored for the stonework.

The waiting rooms were made from acrylic clear sheet with overlays added of plastic sheet and strips. Window frames were drawn as artwork on the computer and made into brass etches. The rather nice entrance porch was constructed in the same way.

MDF was used for the roof sections, with a covering of

Two views of the finished model. The station was built with its own section of platform.

I made up and painted some more stone platform walls, so that the client could make up the rest of the platform length to match mine. A second island platform was also made.

Windows and door made up on acrylic sheet. This is easier to make up, but not so easy when painting all the bars and frames.

The entrance porch makes a nice feature on the model.

plastic sheet. The slates were then glued on in strips as normal. Chimney stacks have wood as a core, covered in brick sheet. The ridge tiles are plastic sheet, cut into a pattern and scored.

Platform bases are softwood supports with MDF on top and plastic sheet was glued on and scored to represent the paving stones. Base wall stones are the Slater's sheets, carefully cut at each joint into a sort of jigsaw pattern, so no vertical join is showing.

The canopies are all plastic construction with an acrylic sheet over the tops for the glazing. I did think about

These pictures show the construction of the model and the base MDF walls. Note the window recesses of the MDF, which have been cut larger than needed, so that the etched frames can be fixed at the correct depth.

32 Kilmacolm Station - *More Model Buildings*

The canopy has been started and the pictures show the construction of it quite clearly.

making the whole lot in brass, but my soldering skills are only just about adequate, so decided that plastic was best for me. The bars have all been cut separately and painted in-situ, which is always a time consuming job, trying not to get paint on the glazing. Valances were drawn up on the computer and brass etches made from this. The glazing was painted in matt varnish, before being weathered.

Notice boards are plastic sheet and strip surrounds with computer artwork signs glued on. Blue enamelled signs were also drawn on the computer and they are fixed in place by drilling small brass rods through the backing and then into the walls.

The model depicts the LMS period.

Walls and all detailing finished. Now waiting for the canopy to be started.

CANAL WHARF
4mm

This commission was totally freelance and designed to fit next to a canal on a layout. I found some pictures in various books and made this model up, using different aspects of them.

As well as the canal, the model was to be located next to a road and the railway. As you can see from the size of this model, I didn't have a lot of space for making a large model, but it still looks OK and it looked good when placed on the layout.

I've used the Slater's large stone sheets for the walls and scored the planking on the doors from plain plastic sheet.

Unfortunately, the pictures I took of it in position on the layout have been lost, when my computer crashed and I hadn't saved them to disc!

LAYOUT FOCUS -
BURNDEN PARK

4mm scale
British Railways period, 1960's

This is not an exhibition layout, but permanently installed at the owner's home. It is based on the Bolton area of Lancashire and many of the buildings and features have been modelled on real ones, found in books of the area. Some of these buildings have long since gone under the bulldozers and new shopping centres and roads.

My first commission for Burnden Park was Bolton Great Moor Street Station, a terminus, which was altered to fit the already-made baseboards. After this first model, many more were commissioned over the next few years, to make a busy station with platforms and canopies and a town scene. As well as the buildings, I have laid some track and landscaped the whole of the layout as well as building new baseboards, with the help of the owner.

Although the layout is fictitious, the owner wanted to portray parts of Bolton that he remembered and so various

Burnden Park terminus station and the end of the canopies.

buildings were made with that in mind. Books were used for reference to find some of the old buildings. As with all models, the research is always a pleasure and it greatly helps in making authentic models.

Over a few years, the layout has been through some changes, as we tried to get the best out of the space available. Some parts were completely taken up and re-built and small add-on baseboards were built with extra scenery.

Now, as I write this book, great changes are being made to Burnden Park. All of the scenes shown here, are no more and the layout has been dismantled and the buildings carefully boxed up. But this is not the end of the Burnden

Although my models are scratchbuilt, I also use other manufacturers materials, when it is needed, especially for scenery. In this picture, I've used setts and fencing, which are both Wills kits.

View of the engine shed from the road bridge. The back yards of the terrace to the right have been made up from the Townstreet Models plaster kits.

36 Burnden Park - *More Model Buildings*

Park layout and I'm pleased to say that the buildings will be placed on a new layout. This layout is larger than the previous one, which is now being constructed in a new home. Quite a few more buildings and different scenery areas need to be made for it.

> **An article on Burnden Park can be seen in British Railway Modelling, August 2007.**

The clock tower in the main street, near the station, tells us the time, which is quite handy for the railway travellers.

Lots of ornate stonework on this model of Yates's Wine Lodge, which was all made up from strips of plastic. The lettering is Slater's alphabet.

> **There is a section on the new Burnden Park layout, after this one. All of the buildings on the old layout have been incorporated in the new design, so the station area is mainly the same as before.**

Part of the carriage sidings, with rows of terraced houses overlooking them.

More Model Buildings - Burnden Park 37

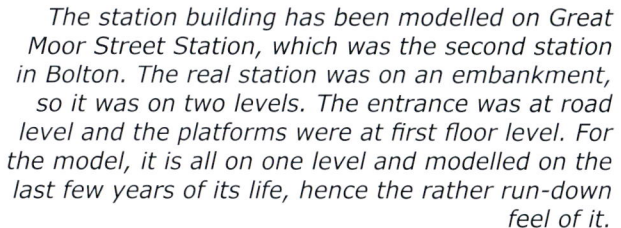

The station building has been modelled on Great Moor Street Station, which was the second station in Bolton. The real station was on an embankment, so it was on two levels. The entrance was at road level and the platforms were at first floor level. For the model, it is all on one level and modelled on the last few years of its life, hence the rather run-down feel of it.

As well as the townscape, the layout had some large areas of countryside, including a canal, spanning the railway.

38 Burnden Park - *More Model Buildings*

From the surrounding countryside, a view of the engine shed is seen. A small car-breakers yard is behind the wooden fence and hoardings. The town is depicted by a ready-printed backscene.

A window-cleaner is busy cleaning a dirty window, in one of the terraces that backs onto the railway.

Burnden Park signal box is a typical LNWR structure. The platforms are just out of sight to the left.

The end of the platforms, with one of the station sign boards. The large corrugated building was modelled from a photograph in a book.

More Model Buildings - Burnden Park 39

In this picture, quite a few of the structures are made from kits. The mill and the cottages are both plaster kits from Townstreet Models. The coal plant is from Ratio and the little chapel is from Wills. This is just an example of using what is available commercially, as well as making scratch-built models.

Another view of the signal box, showing the stairs and station nameboard.

This side of the station building is not normally seen, as it faces the backscene. These days, I model all walls and details if I think a digital camera can get into places to take different pictures.

Terrace backs are always a good idea to model by railway tracks. You can put quite a bit of detailing in place without the scene looking too cluttered.

CONSTRUCTION OF BURNDEN PARK LAYOUT

The entrance to the platforms, with the concourse structure taking shape. This shows how it was made up from plastic sheet and strips. The paving has been scribed onto sheet plastic and I've used brick sheet for the platform surface.

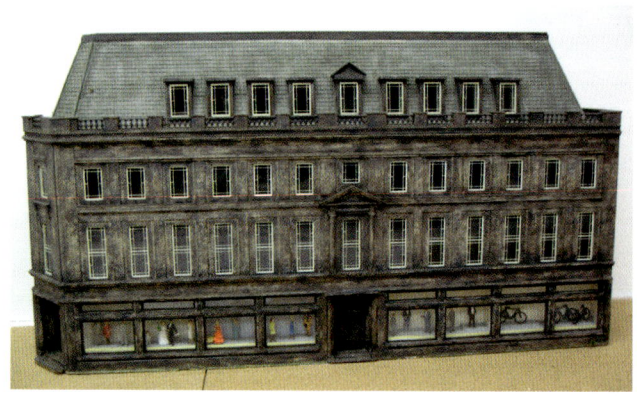

A large department store in the main street. I've use pre-painted figures and bicycles from the Prieser range, for the window displays.

A very early picture of the station platforms. Note the cardboard mock-ups of the buildings in the background.

In contrast to the larger models, I made this up to fit a space. A small corner cafe and warehouse makes it an interesting building.

Left, is the pub and other buildings, grouped on the top of the retaining wall section.

The concourse again with additional platform canopy under construction.

CANAL SCENE

The canal crosses the railway on a girder bridge, made from plastic and etched-brass overlays. This was made up as a separate model and has a painted bed with many layers of varnish applied over the top.

These pictures show how the canal scene was made up. Two main lines come together to form a junction and immediately afterwards, go under the canal bridge and then under the bridge. MDF was used for the main structures and clad in stone and brick sheets.

Compare this picture with the finished scene on page 37.

Here, the two main lines come together to form a junction.

42 Construction of Burnden Park - *More Model Buildings*

Plodder Lane engine shed. The real one was along the line from Great Moor Street.

The countryside section shows the tunnels and rock faces during construction. The rocks have been carved out of very thick plaster, using a chisel, screwdriver and dental probes.

The canopies are well under way and the buildings have appeared at the back of the layout.

View from above the station, showing the engine shed area. New extension baseboards are being made here for the elevated section containing a terrace, made from Townstreet plaster kits. The layout would be changed in other places as well, to try and get the best out of the space available.
Note the backscene, curving towards the viewing area of the station boards. The curved backscene of the scenic section can also be seen here. This is a good idea to get from one scene to another. I first saw this idea on Peter Denny's Buckingham layout, many years ago.

CONSTRUCTION OF NEW BURNDEN PARK LAYOUT

After the dismantling of the old layout, this is proving to be a really nice project; to make a new and improved layout of Burnden Park.

Myself and John Bailey have completely started from scratch, by designing the new layout in its entirety. We've made all the new baseboards and laid new C & L plain track, along with hand-built pointwork, made by John.

The whole layout and track plan was first designed as a 1inch to 1foot drawing on lining paper, before Templot, which is a track design computer programme, was used to get the track flowing properly. It was then printed out on a continuous roll of paper for each section. Apart from the tracks at the platforms of the main station, everything else has been changed from the old track layout.

A lot more space has been given to the engine shed area, which has been brought to the near side of the layout for improved viewing and operation. One thing that wasn't on the old layout, was a goods depot area

These pictures show quite clearly, all the work that still has to be done and the way in which it was started. Lots of mock-ups can be seen and they are being replaced as the models are finished. Some of the buildings at the station end you will recognize from the old layout.

Note the new engine shed area, which now has a coaling stage. A turntable will be installed to the left of the coaling stage.

At this stage of construction, anything can happen, so buildings might get changed around, before we are completely satisfied with the design. It has now been decided not to keep the mill in this scene and other buildings will take its place.

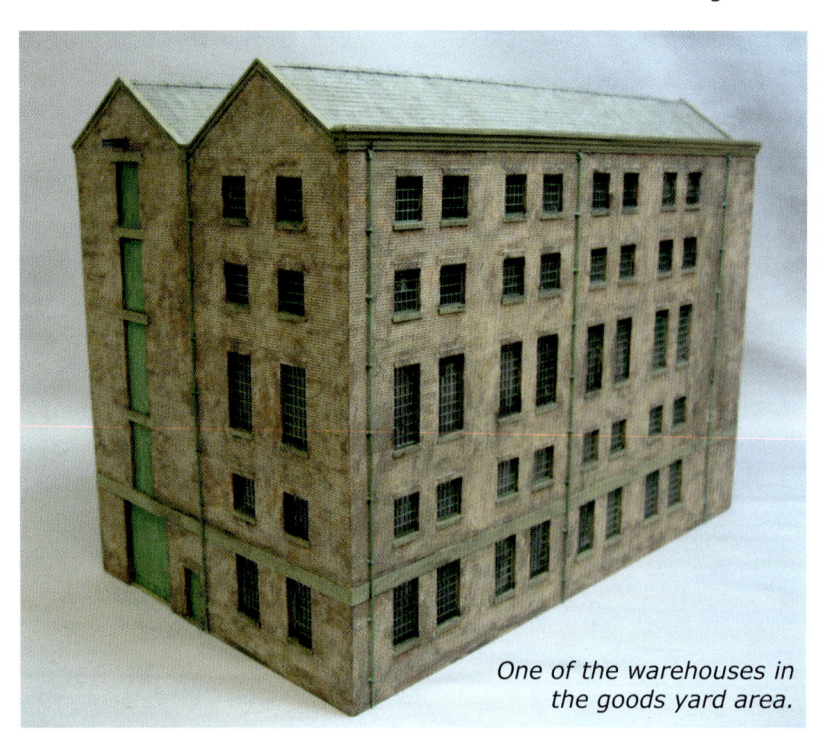

44 Construction of New Burnden Park - *More Model Buildings*

and so one has been added, with a parcels and goods warehouse, along with some other warehouses. More buildings have been made, as the area given to the main station baseboard, is a lot longer than before.

Again, backscenes are used to come across the width of the layout to make separate scenes. The layout now has four separate scenes, which are:- a viaduct scene, a junction station scene, a branch station scene and of course the terminus station scene. A new storage yard with traverser has also been built.

The pictures show how the layout is being built and the usual mock-ups are there to get a feel of what we want to achieve.

One of the warehouses in the goods yard area.

The new goods warehouse, made in low-relief to fit at the back of the goods sidings. It actually tapers, at an angle from left to right, which makes it look better than being parallel to the backscene. The lettering was first set on the computer and printed off. Each letter was carefully cut out to form a stencil, taped to the wall and the outline pencilled in. The letters were then carefully painted with white paint and weathered.

More Model Buildings - Construction of New Burnden Park 45

Signal Box No. 2, built in the LNWR style.

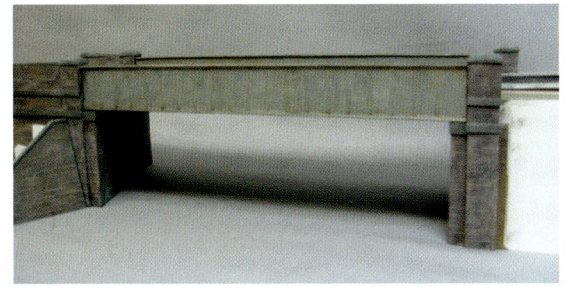

It was decided to make a new bridge for the town scene, as it would now go over the tracks at an angle, so I chose to make a girder structure with brick pillars. I've made the road a little bit wider than the previous one.

The second of the warehouse buildings has a corrugated iron walkway, which will join both of them up.

A new viaduct, ready to be put in place.

This is one of the many signals for the layout, built by Tony Gee.

The coaling stage is based on the one formerly at Bolton. It has been made complete, on its own sub-baseboard, with ramp and elevated track for the coal wagons.

TERRACE, GOODS SHED AND WATER TOWER
4mm

This terrace was modelled on one picture found in a book of Todmorden, West Yorkshire. It was right in the background and difficult to really get the feel of it. As you can see, it is on a hill, so the model had to be made accordingly.

The water tower is a freelance model, but based on one that could be found in quite a few areas. The water is just a few coats of varnish on a painted base.

A freelance model of a long goods shed, with loading bay and small office.

More Model Buildings - Hotel and Footbridge 47

HOTEL AND FOOTBRIDGE
4mm

This is another freelance model with a nice portico entrance.

It is of basic construction methods, with divider walls for strengthening. Brick sheet has been applied with stonework details.

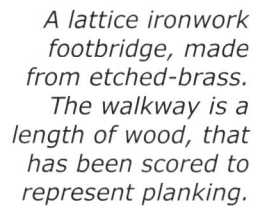

A lattice ironwork footbridge, made from etched-brass. The walkway is a length of wood, that has been scored to represent planking.

LAYOUT FOCUS -
MILTON HALL

7mm scale
British Railways period, 1960's

This is another privately owned layout, so is not on the exhibition circuit. It is based loosely on the North Eastern area in BR days. All the buildings have been constructed by myself over a few years and although some are freelance, they have various elements of the real buildings represented.

On the layout, there are three stations including a terminus called Milton Hall, which is the main and largest one. Alton is also a terminus and, finally, Lingdale, the island platform station. There is also a disused island station with bridge, a colliery, two engine sheds, a working coaling plant, two goods sheds, three signal boxes and various mess rooms and huts.

Part of the station nearing completion on my workbench. The roof to the left has been made, but owing to the large size of the model, I couldn't put it all up at the same time. The wires seen here are for the lights and they were later fixed to go down the columns and through the platforms.

Being in the larger scale of 7mm, some models are very large and the terminus station of Milton Hall is a good example. The building of them consists of a slightly different approach to the smaller scales, in as much as the base material is usually MDF (medium density fibreboard) of different thicknesses.

The research has been interesting again and I have purchased a few books on the North Eastern region area, for inspiration.

All interior details were added, such as the ticket barriers and poster and timetable hoardings.

ALTON STATION

This is the second terminus station on the layout and quite a bit smaller than the main station. The low-relief building has a lovely reddish-brown stone colouring with light stone surrounds. It has been based on Kirkby Stephen Station in Cumbria.

The columns, which have been made from a master, have been cast in brass.

More Model Buildings - Milton Hall, Alton Station 51

Alton Station is a low-relief model with a full canopy. The second island platform, shown here, also has a canopy. Lots of etched-brass for the brackets and canopy glazing bars was needed.

A coaling plant with conveyor. This was a really nice model to make. Lots of corrugated sheeting with plenty of weathering.

> **Corrugated sheeting can be painted in various ways. One way is to paint the sheeting first with the rust colour (I use Humbrol 62). The final colour can then be painted on top, but not covering all the rust up. Weathering powders, used sparingly, can also be added to the final finish.**
> **Another way is to paint it normally and dry-brush the rust paint on in patches.**

More Model Buildings - Milton Hall

The stone-built engine shed, was made from carving DAS modelling clay.

Both the waiting room and the platform, on Lingdale station, are of the more modern concrete design, which makes a nice contrast to the other buildings.

The rather elegant looking Milton Hall signal cabin.

Back part of the Northlight engine shed, made to look like the roof had been taken off at some stage.

The main coaling plant is a working model. Although I did quite a lot of the work, such as some details and all the painting etc., a few others also had a lot of input into the model, especially with the mechanism. The working part of it was dificult to make and it took some time to achieve the end result.

COLLIERY

The pit-head winding wheels show up nicely here, along with all the girders.

The winding house and chimney.

The colliery, which was made on its own baseboard, was a big project to make and a little awkward, as it was to be built on a curve.

The main buildings are the pit-head tower, engine winding house, lorry hoppers and screens. Also, there are filler buildings and corrugated conveyors. The chimney is a cast plaster kit and apart from the wheels themselves, which were made by someone else, everything else, I scratch-built.

Lighting was added to most of the buildings, so some thoughts were needed on where the wiring would go.

The lorry hoppers, can accommodate up to four lorries.

More Model Buildings - Milton Hall, Colliery 55

The screens, with one of the corrugated conveyors, just in view.

The base of the pit-head.

CONSTRUCTION OF MILTON HALL - MILTON HALL STATION

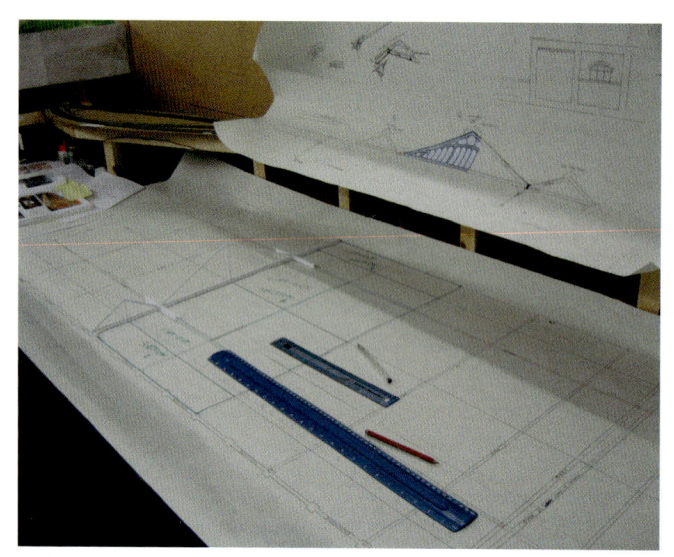

Full scale plans were drawn up of the canopies. The tracks were already laid, so it was important to get the measurements right.

Painting the retaining wall. The part to the left has had extra dry-brushing applied.

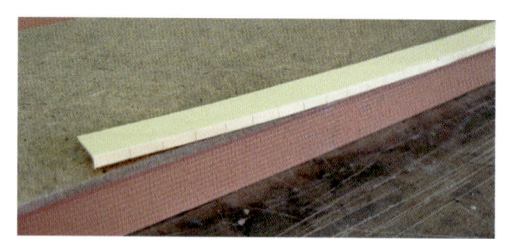

Covering the platform edges in plastic brick and edging stones, made from thin card.

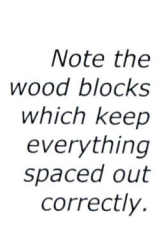

Note the wood blocks which keep everything spaced out correctly.

It's all beginning to take shape now, with the retaining wall and columns in place. The roof girders were made up in a jig, so they would all be identical. Only the main canopy and one side canopy could be erected at one time, due to space restriction on the workbench.

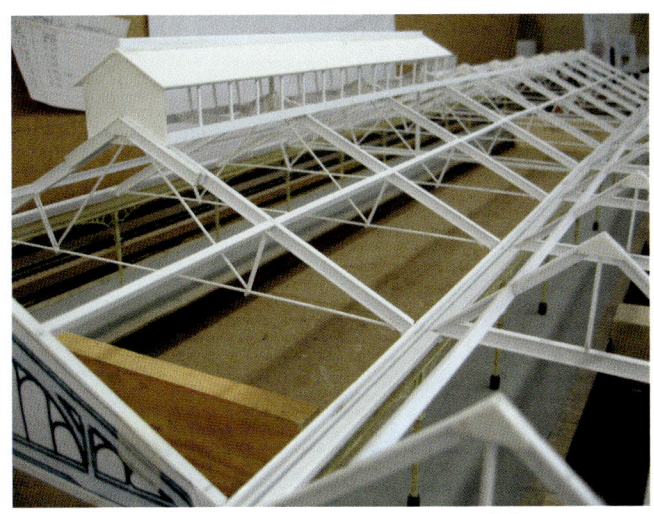

More Model Buildings - Construction of Milton Hall 57

Girders are now in place and also part of the main smoke vent is being worked on.

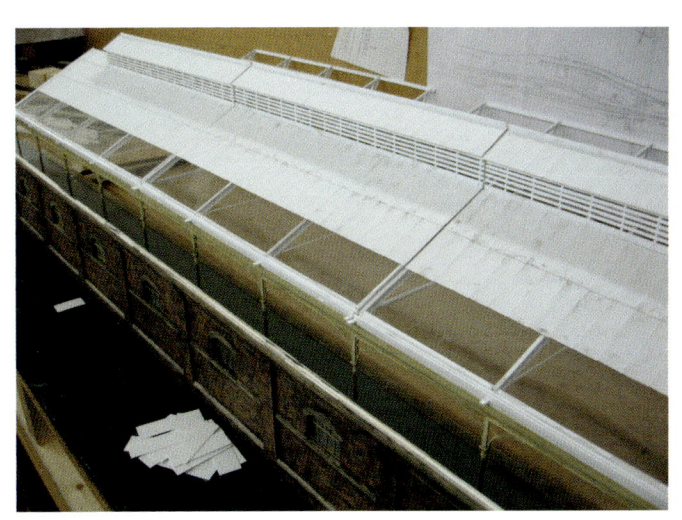

Corrugated sheets have been fixed over the sheet of glazing material, which covers the whole roof.

This is the main central canopy, now with the glazing screen attached. This has been etched out of brass in two halves.

The station was made up into sections, making it easier to construct and transport. However, this can cause problems hiding the joins when you are re-assembling.

Each column has an excess piece on the base, which fits into holes drilled in the platform.

This is the other side of the station canopy and instead of a brick wall, it has a wood valance, supported on columns. Note the base that it fits onto, so it is easier to place on the layout and fix in place.

CONSTRUCTION OF MILTON HALL - COLLIERY

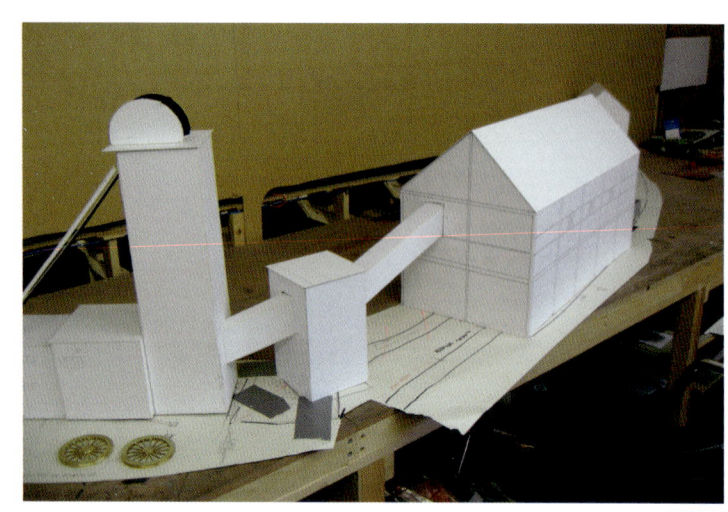

Mock-up buildings are a very useful way of ensuring that the model you are going to make actually fits the space and, just as importantly, whether they look right. It is easier to change anything at this stage, before construction begins.

The mock-ups for the colliery were essential to get the right look, especially as the baseboard was on a curve and not very wide. You can see the main features here and also the winding wheels, which were later replaced with better ones.

The view looking down on the pit head buildings, shows how I constructed them. Note also, the paper plan underneath, which was cut to follow the tracks on the layout. The top deck is seen here, with the cut outs for both wheels and a cut out for steps down to the next level.

As the hoppers inside the screens had to be a working model, I had to build two of them and get them just right. The measured amount of coal was poured in at the top of the building, falling down the hoppers and making two mounds in each wagon.

More Model Buildings - Construction of Colliery 59

The tower is taking shape and the girders are being added and painted. The steps have yet to be constructed up one of the legs, which was a very time consuming job.

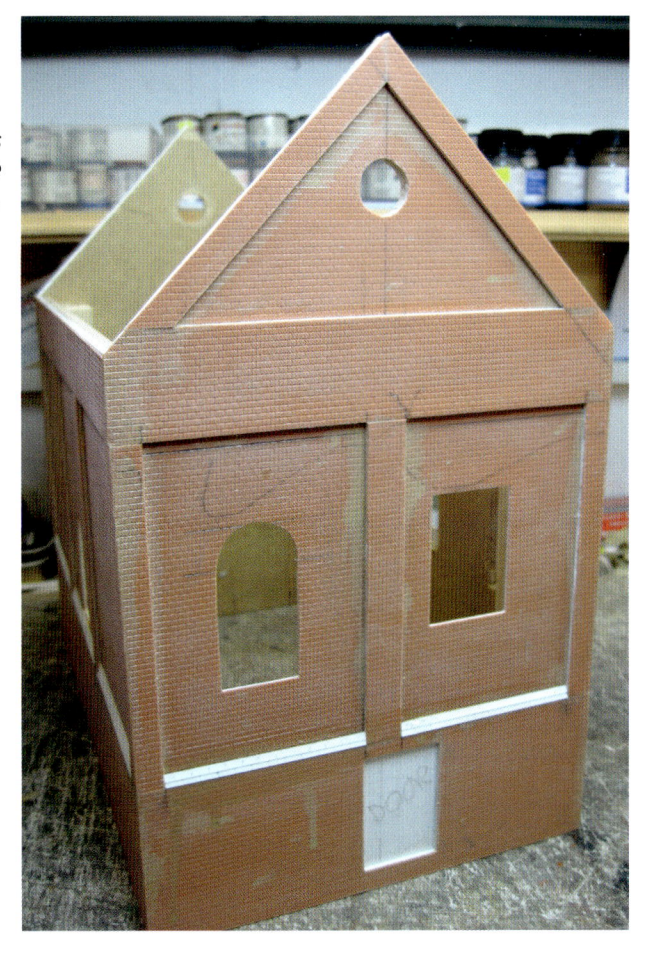

The Winding house now has bricks and plinths added. This will house a motor to operate the wires for the wheels.

The platform can be seen, which will have a narrow gauge track for the tubs to come out from the pit head.

60 Construction of Colliery - *More Model Buildings*

The screens, showing before and after the painting. The hoppers, for pouring the coal down, are at the top of the roof, at the back.

The top of the roof shows the two hoppers for pouring in the coal.

One of the corrugated structures for the conveyor belts. Always a great painting job to represent well worn and rusty corrugated iron.

The lorry hoppers model was a nice one to make. In real life, the hoppers would be operated by pulling down on a chain to let the coal out into the lorry. I've used some fine chain for this feature, but it is not a working model.

CONSTRUCTION OF
MILTON HALL - NORTHLIGHT ENGINE SHED

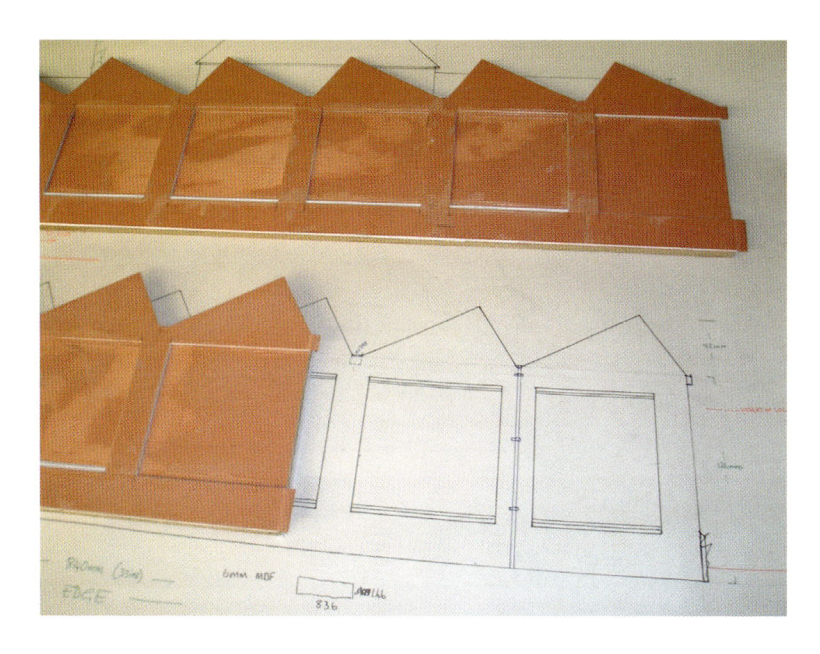

I found a very similar shed in a book, so thought it would be a nice for a change, to model something without a roof. MDF was used for the base material, with a covering of plastic sheet, followed by the bricks and plinths. I drew up scale plans to make sure enough clearances would be available for engines to enter the shed, before commencing with the model. The girders and columns have been made up from plastic, with etched-brass brackets.

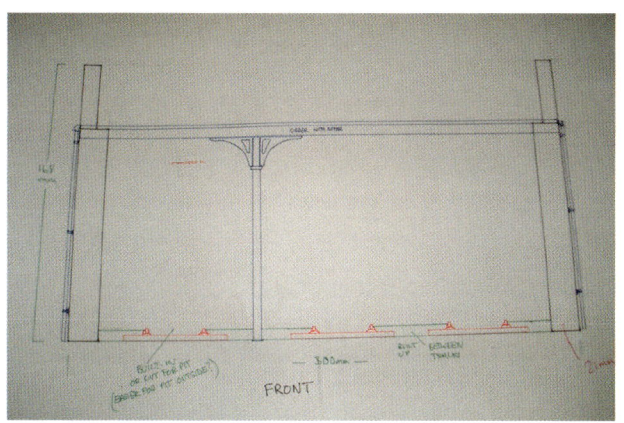

CONSTRUCTION OF MILTON HALL - ALTON STATION

This is a low-relief model, being only about 50mm in width. It is based on Kirkby Stephen station building, as I liked the ornate stone surrounds to the windows and doorways.

Again, it is MDF based, with DAS modelling clay attached with a thin coating of PVA adhesive. After thoroughly being allowed to dry for a week, the

MDF wall cut out, with the resin surrounds glued in place. These had plastic strips under them, to get them to the right height, when the clay was attached to the wall.

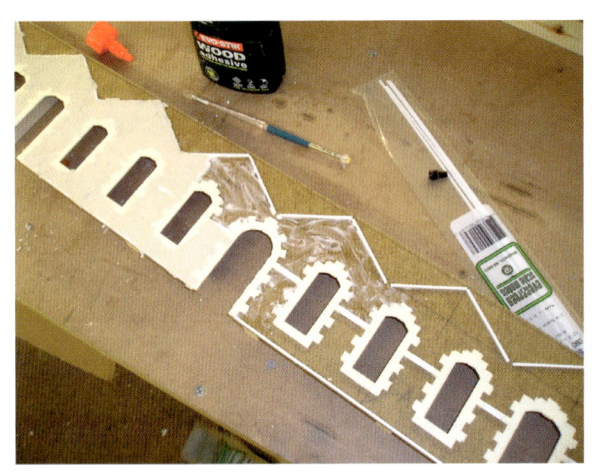

DAS clay being applied to a smearing of PVA glue.

The wall is completelly covered with clay and needs a week to thoroughly dry.

Rubber moulds for windows and doors. I had to make one master for each item in full, to make all this work properly.

The finished, carved and painted wall.

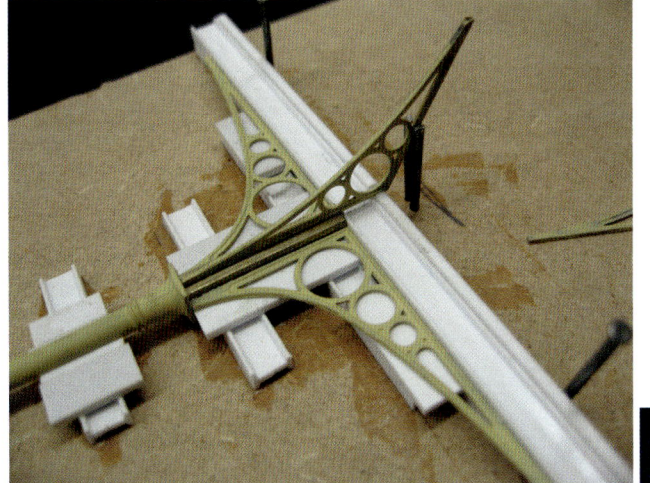

More Model Buildings - Construction of Alton Station

I made a jig up to enable me to get each column, complete with brackets, to look identical and square. At the same time, I glued a cross girder in place. It was a very crude jig, but one that worked. You can see nails to hold the girder in place and two more nails to keep the canopy bracket up, while waiting for the super-glue to set hard.

A completed island platform canopy section, which has been soldered together.

Both platform canopies can be seen here and note the extra base on each column, for fixing into holes in the platform. It's easier to paint items like these, if they are temporarily fixed onto scrap wood pieces

long process of carving individual stones could begin.

From these pictures, you can see how I made the walls up from MDF and the modelling clay. The rubber moulds for casting identical window and door surrounds, were a great help and it was worth the extra cost involved in buying the rubber and resin mixes.

For the canopy columns, I had a master made and then had castings done from that. All the rest of the canopy sections and brackets were from my own artwork, which were made into etched-brass.

Compare these pictures with the finished model on pages 50 and 51.

> **Resin has a shelf life of approximately six months, so try and use it up with other moulds for different models.**

Some of the parts needed for the canopy

BRIDGE FOR BUCKFASTLEIGH

This road bridge will be placed on a layout, modelled on Buckfastleigh. Only the middle arch has a track through it, hence the soot deposits on the stones above it.

A retaining wall was made at the same time and the joint to the bridge will be filled neatly when in place.

The construction is fairly straightforward, using plastic for the base and then a layer of DAS modelling clay over the top. After thoroughly drying, the clay was carved into stonework and then painted, using Humbrol enamel paints.

> When applying DAS to plastic, still use a smearing of PVA glue first, but when dry, apply MEK liquid cement all round the apertures. This should ensure that everything bonds well.

The bottom two pictures show the basic structure made from 40thou plastic. The roadway is thick card with a coating of pva and weathering powders rubbed into it. Various black and grey washes finished it off.

PLATFORMS FOR BUCKFASTLEIGH

I mostly make platforms with good quality card bases and a card top. The walls are cut first and spacers are glued to one side with PVA glue, before adding the second side.

Plastic stone sheet was glued on with a thin layer of Evo-stik impact glue. To get a continuous stone side, I cut into the mortar courses and make a jigsaw end. Milliput can be used to fill any gaps. The pictures show how this is achieved.

Edging stones were cut into the card and as the surface was tarmac, then nothing else had to be done, other than the painting. If it had been flagstones, then they would have had to be cut into the card as well.

This shows how I cut the stone sheet to get the jigsaw end.

> **For painting card models, such as platform surfaces and slate roofs, I usually dilute the Humbrol enamels, with a few drops of thinners. This makes the paint flow better over the surface. You can always go over it with another coat later.**

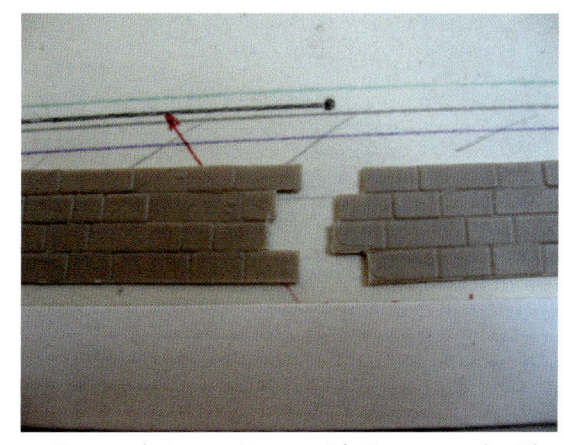

Dressed stone pieces with jigsaw ends. The larger stones make the job a bit easier.

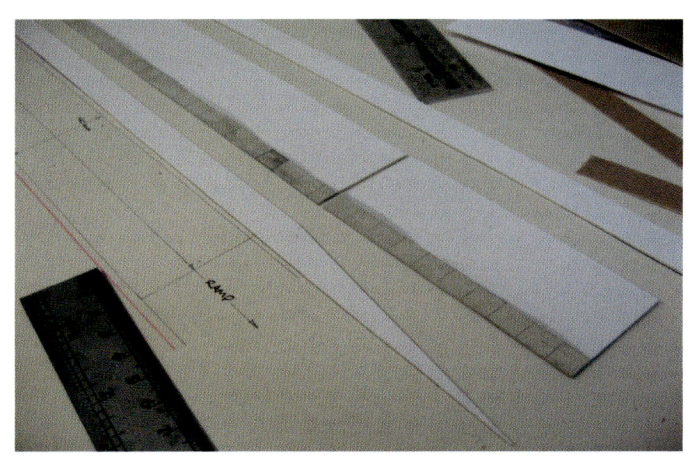

Edging stones on the platform surface have been scribed and painted. Note the side card wall with ramp.

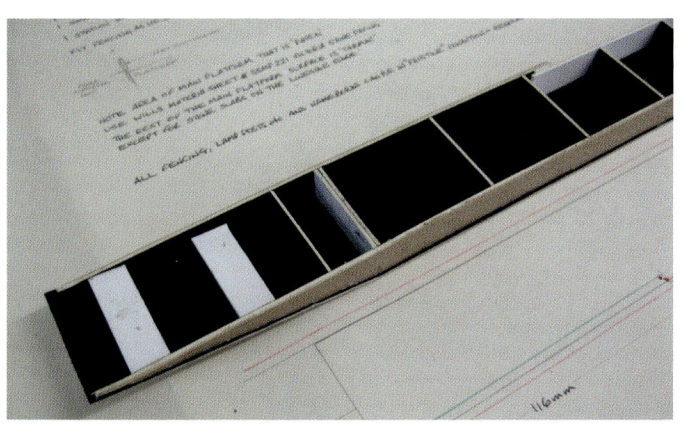

Underneath of the platform, showing the card formers.

The platform is about six feet long and was made to be in one piece, using card joiners. If the card top is cut to stagger the joint, then the model becomes quite sturdy.

LAYOUT FOCUS -
EDGWARE ROAD
UNDER CONSTRUCTION
4mm scale

The layout, which is being constructed, is based on the London area, around Paddington in 1945/6, so is in GWR colours. Due to war-time hostilites, the glazing was taken out from the canopy roof and painting and general cleaning was not done, so everything would be very dirty. None of the trackwork and baseboards have been done by myself, but so far, I've built the terminus station, a signal box and a bridge.

I drew up the full-sized plan from measurements that the client had given to me. It has a two roofed canopy spanning five tracks, which has been entirely made from plastic sheet, strips and plastic girders. The canopy and waiting rooms have been based on the one at Henley-on-Thames, but this one has two canopies, side by side. To get the middle columns located down the centre of the platform, I had to make each roof with different widths.

The model was all made on a temporary MDF base, with

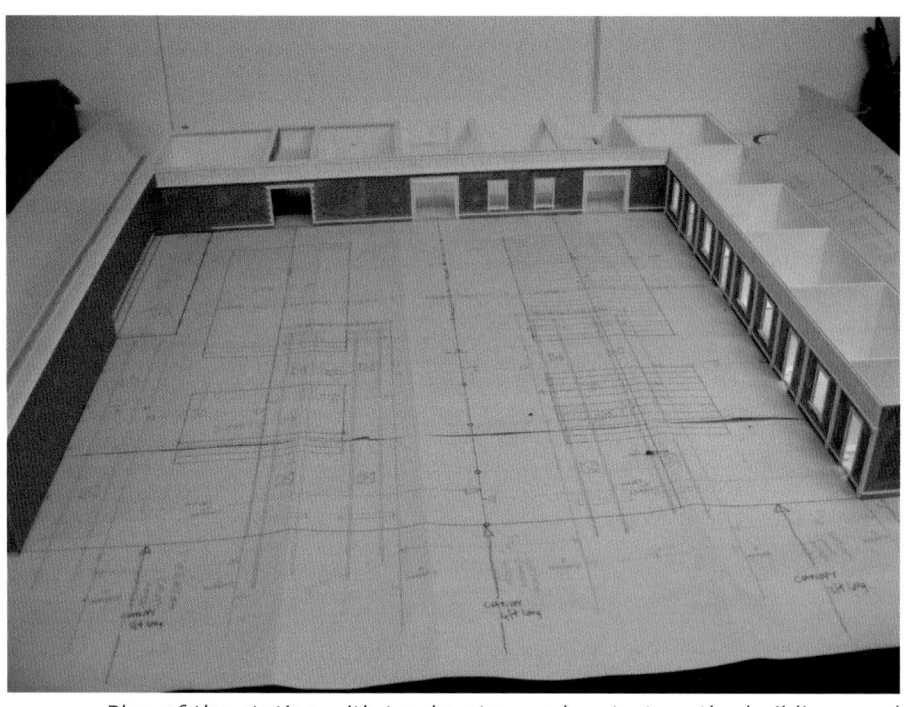

Plan of the station with tracks etc., and a start on the buildings and retaining wall is well underway.

You can see all the work that had to be done on the underside of one of the roofs. Although it might never be seen, I scored the planking as well.

More Model Buildings - Edgware Road 67

The main buildings have been finished and painted and the canopy structure is well advanced.

The first of the two canopies is in place and also the central columns. Note the MDF board and wood blocks, which I made the model on. I've marked it out with all tracks and platforms, so I have a guide where eveything fits.

68 Edgware Road - *More Model Buildings*

The signal box is a typical Great Western design and based on Westbury box. Construction is a brick base, with wood framing for the top part. A lever frame kit, from Springside Models, was made, painted and glued in position, along with the usual instrument shelf, desks, notice boards and a fireplace.

wood blocks around three sides to enable me to get the correct width of the building. The model is not viewed from the entrance side of the building, so that part wasn't modelled. It is made up of two main buildings, one of which is the entrance hall with ticket office and the other one is for waiting rooms and lamp rooms etc. A retaining wall goes down the whole length of one side, with a small flat roofed building at the end.

I did some artwork on the computer for the iron railings and gates, which I am particularly pleased with. Most signs shown here, were also drawn on the computer. The platform number signs were fixed to a brass rod that goes across the whole width of the inside, and is located in holes in the walls.

The etched-brass iron gates and railings have come out well. These are only just propped up on the board and as you can see, one isn't!

After fixing the station building down, some rolling stock was placed on the tracks. The iron railings and the gates have also been glued in place.

More Model Buildings - Edgware Road 69

Lots of detail here, with the underside of the canopy roof with all its trusses and the decorative supports at the top of the walls. The flat-roofed building is to the left and just showing, is the rod and tube that holds the platform numbers in place across the whole width of the concourse. The smoke troughs and vents are clearly seen here and they will be over the tracks, when the model is placed on the layout.

Another picture of the inside of the station, after being placed on the layout. The different areas of light, coming in from the canopy, make a nice effect.

The slender chimneys give the roof an elegant character.

BRICK TERRACES WITH PUB
4mm

This model was designed to fit a corner space on a layout. It is a freelance model, so it is not based on any particular terrace.

Basically, it is two terraces, one of which is modelled fully, while the other one has only been modelled showing the backs. This is because the front of it will be positioned up against the backscene.

There is a small pub at one end of the full terrace and the

The whole model was built on a base, which enabled me to do a bit of scenery as well.

More Model Buildings - Brick Terraces with Pub 71

The pub signs were drawn on the computer.

Curtains are cut from the pages of a catalogue. Don't use large patterns, but keep to the plainer ones.

yards and outhouses have been made complete for both terraces. An alleyway goes through the front terrace and into the yards and the back of the pub. The whole model was made on its own base, which makes it easier to put in all the vegetation and also, easier to bed the buildings in, when placed on a layout.

Construction for these terraces was straightforward. Brick sheet was applied to the walls and the outhouses were built up as separate units and fixed to the main walls.

# THREE BRIDGES ENGINE SHED
4mm

This three-road engine shed was situated on the London to Brighton main line at Crawley and built in 1911.

Pictures were sent to me of the different sides and from those, I drew up scale plans, before commencing work on the model. Lots of brick counting was needed, as no sizing was given. No roof glazing was needed, so both sides of the roof are slated. It has a water tower and mess rooms attached to the shed wall, which gives it a lot of character.

For the model, I have used a base plastic of 40thou thickness, which helps keep the model more sturdy.

These pictures show how each part was made and painted.

More Model Buildings - Three Bridges Engine Shed 73

Part of one of the sides, cut from 40thou sheet.

Bricks have been added to one side leaving a space for the mess rooms.

The plinth overlays have now been added and also the cills and lintels.

The water tower has been made and the walls cemented together with spacing girders.

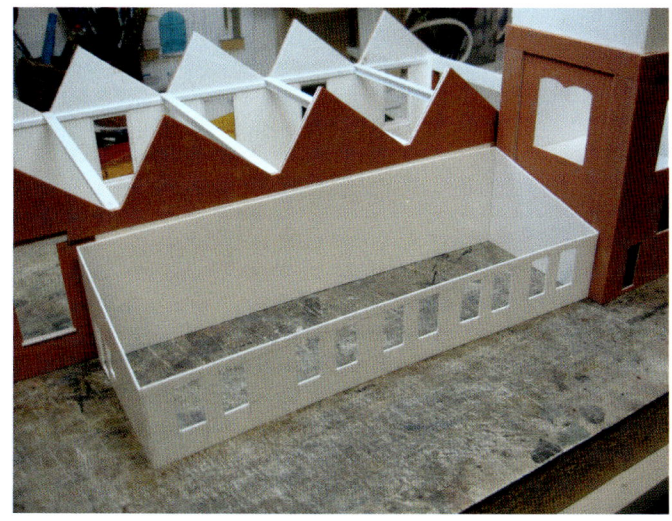

Mess rooms being worked on and placed to make sure it fits against the wall and tower.

The first painting of the base colour, which will be a yellowish brick, but well-weathered.

Three Bridges Engine Shed - *More Model Buildings*

Girders made to keep the width of the shed accurate.

Girders now have a plastic base over them, so that the roof can be constructed. Formers were made for this.

Smoke vents added and all base roofs are made.

Card slates, cut into strips and worked from the bottom of the roof, working upwards.

The first coat of paint is slightly thinned, so it is not put on too thickly and filling the tiny cuts between slates.

The water tower just has its tank to be finished, but lots of detail still to be done, such as drainpipes, etc.

More Model Buildings - Three Bridges Engine Shed   75

The chimney has just been finished and is now ready for painting. It will be glued to the water tower wall and any gaps will be filled with Milliput.

The water tank now has a corrugated roof

The chimney has been attached to the wall, with the gaps being filled with Milliput.

The roof of the tank has been painted and the vents will need their individual roofs attached.

LAYOUT FOCUS -
WHITECHAPEL
UNDER CONSTRUCTION

4mm scale
Victorian period, 1890's

This layout is still under construction, although the trackwork is finished (not made by myself). I've been asked to make the buildings and walls for this, quite different layout to my usual models, set in London's East End in the late Victorian era, circa 1890's.

It is a freelance layout of the Great Eastern Railway, but based on elements in the area. The buildings are being modelled from photographs or ones that are still standing today.

The track is on an embankment throughout and ends in

The two station buildings have loads of character and, as in those far off days, had various displays of posters and advertising which decorated the walls.

Well advanced here, with most of the decorative stonework in place.

a terminus station. It has four platform faces and on street level, there are two different station buildings, serving two different railway companies. The railway companies are the East London Railway and the Metropolitan District Railway. The passengers would have quite a few steps to reach the platforms, after buying their tickets.

Although most of my models are scratch-built, now and again, I'm asked to make up kits for the owners of the layouts. For Whitechapel, I was asked to make long lengths of the Wills walls and paint and weather them. I carefully measured the lengths needed and constructed them in easy to manage sections, so that they would slot together when placed in position.

The backs of the station buildings here, are at platform level and contrast greatly to the ornate frontages. The steps from the pavement just go up to a side door in one of the buildings. This platform side will eventually have a canopy attached to it.

The entrance to the East London Railway station platforms.

More Model Buildings - Whitechapel 79

I've also constructed two warehouses, one being on the embankment and the other on baseboard level They are joined up by a corrugated walkway.

One of the platforms has got a full canopy and this is scratch-built. We found one photograph in a book that would be in keeping and so I've more or less copied the style of it. It's mostly made from etched-brass, which I've drawn on the computer first. What stands out about it is the lovely curved awnings. There are three different brackets under the canopy and the last four bays are on a curved platform on one side.

A floor plan of the platform was sent to me and I was given a possible length of the canopy. From this, I drew up the design and structure and then went ahead to construct it.

A column was drawn up to scale and a picture was sent with it, to get a master made and then white metal castings were cast from that.

I also drew up the canopy glazing bars, which were made into brass etches.

Apart from various plastic strips and sheet, the other main material used was the Plastruct girders for holding up the canopy on the columns.

Painting was applied in green and light cream and then quite heavily weathered, especially on the canopy tops and glazing.

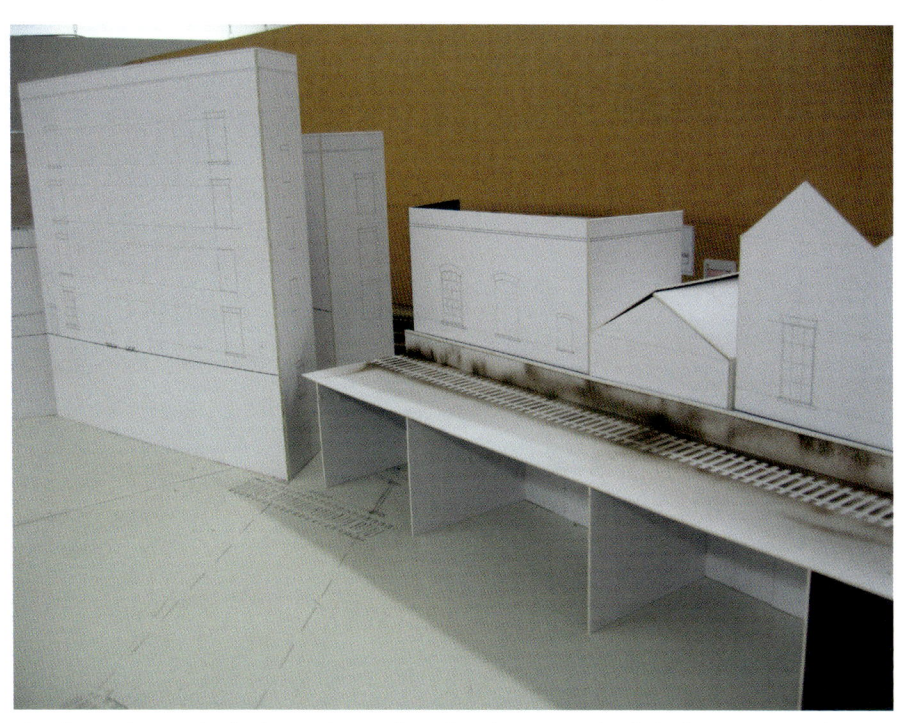

Card mock-ups include a piece of embankment, which helps to get a better feel of what I was attempting to achieve.

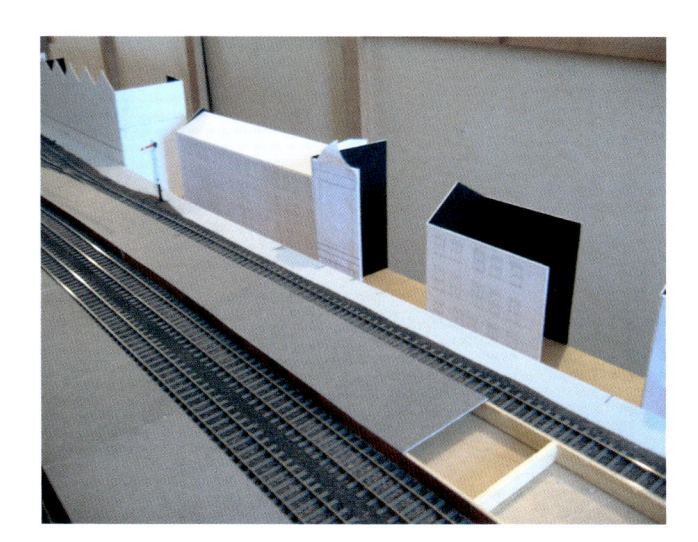

The mock-ups are arranged right along the back of the layout and are mostly low-relief models. Some of the fine trackwork is shown here.

80 Whitechapel - *More Model Buildings*

The brickwork has had its first coat of paint applied. Dry-brushing will be the next job, using various colours, until it resembles proper bricks.

The two warehouses with the corrugated walkway that spans a single track. The blocks of wood are at embankment height and it is a good way of seeing how models will look when in position.

The corrugated walkway was made longer than needed, so that when the buildings are in place, it can be slid either way into holes, cut in to the sides of the buildings. Once in place on the layout, that gap above the walkway can be filled.

CANOPY

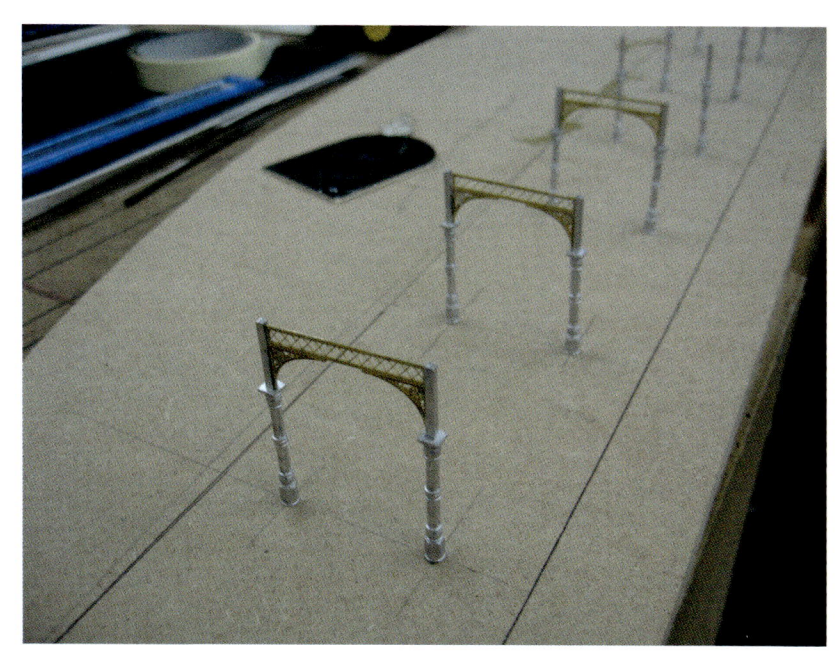

The canopy had to fit the platform exactly, so the measurements given were followed closely.

An outline of the platform edge was drawn on 12mm MDF and marked where the columns would be located. You can see how I marked these up, using a set-square and long ruler to get the correct positions. Holes were then drilled accurately in these centres to locate the extra base on the columns. As I was only using this MDF to get positioning, I wouldn't be glueing anything in place, as it had to be lifted out when finished.

I had designed the centre girder etch, complete with brackets, to be in one piece. This enabled me to keep the spacing between columns the same all the way along. These were all fixed together with super-glue.

All the etched-brass brackets are double-sided, which gives them more strength and shows the detail both sides.

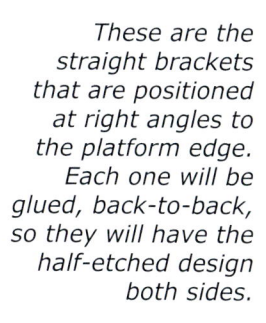

Angled roof brackets attached to the columns.

These are the straight brackets that are positioned at right angles to the platform edge. Each one will be glued, back-to-back, so they will have the half-etched design both sides.

82 Whitechapel - *More Model Buildings*

All the brackets have been glued in place and now the Plastruct girders have been cut to fit and located on the width. Each girder was drilled to accept long brass rods, which go all the way down the length of the canopy. Using a set-square to keep the columns upright, the rod was super-glued to each girder. This really helped to keep the structure together and will be handy to fix lamps on when they are ready.

Roof girders are now being fixed to the other ones.

It is now taking shape with all girders in place. Corrugated sheets have been added at the bottom half of each bay. The lovely etched-brass valancing has also been glued in place, which makes a huge difference to the structure.

Everything has been given a coat of primer and is now ready for painting.

More Model Buildings - Whitechapel 83

The finished model, now painted and weathered. Note the glazing is semi see-through. To get this result, I coat the clear glazing with matt varnish and then it is heavily weathered, using a thinned down black wash.

Just the hanging lamps to fix and the model is fully completed.

It is easier to paint everything first, before attaching any glazing. This stops any paint from getting onto the glazing, which will be hard to remove.

The canopy is now in place on the platform, complete with hanging lamps. Also in the picture, are the waiting rooms and stairs down to the underpass, for access to the other platform. Still bits to tidy up on the platforms and the retaining wall needs fixing in place.

FOUNTAIN HOTEL
4mm

The Fountain Hotel is located in Cowes, on the Isle of Wight. It is rather an ornate building, with a steeply-pitched roof and tall chimney stacks.

Only the front and side walls have been modelled and I didn't need to model the back wall, as it will be up against the backscene. All the walls are rendered, so no bricks needed to be glued on. This was achieved with the wet paint and talcum powder method. See the box on page 86, which explains the way in which I achieve this.

Two of the first-floor windows have semi-circular mouldings above them, as does the entrance doorway. These were measured up, drawn on the computer and made into brass etches.

The basic shell has been made and the two different front walls have been glued together.

> **When adding dormer windows to a model, make the window with reasonable lengths of side and top walls. This will enable you to position the module on the base of the roof and cut the sloping roof to fit it.**

Semi-circular mouldings have been fixed in place together with the bay window frames.

This is one of the corner stone lengths. It has been scored across for the individual stones and I've now started the cutting out of the parts not needed. When this is finished, it will be scored down the back in the centre, until the whole piece can be bent at right-angles to fit around the corner.

The corner stones show up well here and the first part of the outside moulding has been done.

86 Fountain Hotel - *More Model Buildings*

The steeply-pitched roof, with dormer windows and the tall chimney stacks give this model character.

Passage-way through the building to the back yard. The bay window is a nice feature.

> **Rendered walls are fairly straighforward to achieve. Put one coat of paint on first and let it dry thoroughly. The second coat is then applied and while it is still wet, sprinkle talcum powder on to it. Shake it around and lightly blow over it. Don't attempt to try and brush excess powder off at this stage, as it will ruin the effect. The final painting can be done when all is dry. This is done by stippling (not brushing), another coat of paint on to the wall, until the powder has been covered.**

Close-up of the window surrounds and inner mouldings.

The rendered wall is my usual method of talcum powder stippled onto the wet paint.

TREES

To make a convincing looking tree is harder than it looks, especially if you want it to look right. I have seen some really nice trees on layouts at exhibitions, but in general, a lot of them don't look very convincing.

These trees are the only ones I've made from scratch and it was quite time consuming.

They were made from galvanised wire strands twisted together and glued with a hot glue gun. Then a plaster and pva mix was applied over the frame.

The trunks and branches were sprayed with browns and greys, then a black wash brushed on, to get into the crevices. Woodlands scenic matting and foam particles were placed over branches that had spots of pva glue on them.

WALLS

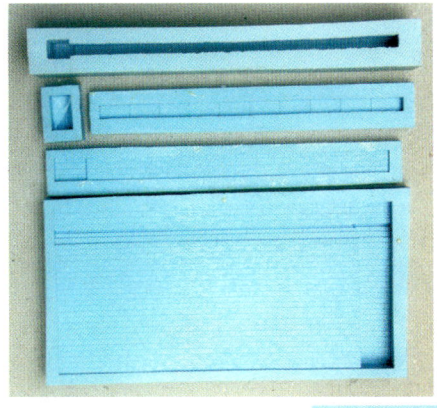

This wall could either be a large one in 4mm scale or a smallish one in 7mm, so either would be OK.

I made a master, from plastic, for each part and formed boxes to pour liquid rubber into. These were left to harden for a week before I could use the moulds. Then resin was poured into the rubber moulds and in a few minutes, after it hardened, they could be taken out carefully. If I did this wall again, the pillar would be separate from the main wall, so not so much rubber would be used.

The set of rubber moulds above, which make the retaining wall. The very top one is a low wall, which is a separate mould.

The finished and painted wall, using two sets of resin castings.

ST. MARY'S CHURCH
4mm

This church is in Todmorden, West Yorkshire and from my own photographs and sketches taken on site, drawings were made to scale. These plans were then drawn on 30thou plastic sheet and all apertures cut out.

All stonework on this model was hand scribed on to the plastic walls. Overlays for the window and door surrounds were made from sheet and strips. The large corner stones were made up as one piece for each corner and scored down the back until they could be bent at right angles.

The model was actually made in two parts; the tower and the main building. Both of them were complete with windows and doors and both were painted before being cemented together.

The windows were drawn as artwork and made into brass etches. The louvred openings on the tower have separate pieces of strip and the clock face was drawn on the computer and has etched hands from the Scale Link range. The weather vane is also a Scale Link etch.

The groundwork for the graveyard was made up of plaster over card and polystyrene formers. Rocks were carved out of the thick plaster using a chisel and various dental probes. The stone steps, from the gate to the church doors, were moulded and carved from Milliput. Fencing is from Scale Link but the very fine entrance gates are my own artwork, which was made into brass etches.

The top picture is the main wall with all details added and stones scribed. The next picture down has the tower and main part temporarily attached and the painting has begun.

Close-up of the wall showing the base colour and the dry-brushing colours gradually being worked across the model, from left to right.

The painting of the tower has been finished. Note the louvre window and the clockface.

90 St. Mary's Church - *More Model Buildings*

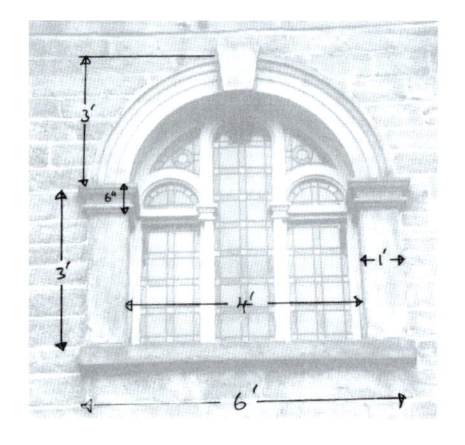

One of the best ways to get measurements of a building and its windows and doors, is to take photographs and then tape an overlay of tracing paper over the top. Measurements can then be written on without spoiling the photograph. These photographs were taken before digital photography, but you could still use the same method now.

You can also see that I've done the same for the corner stones and widths and heights of some of the walls.

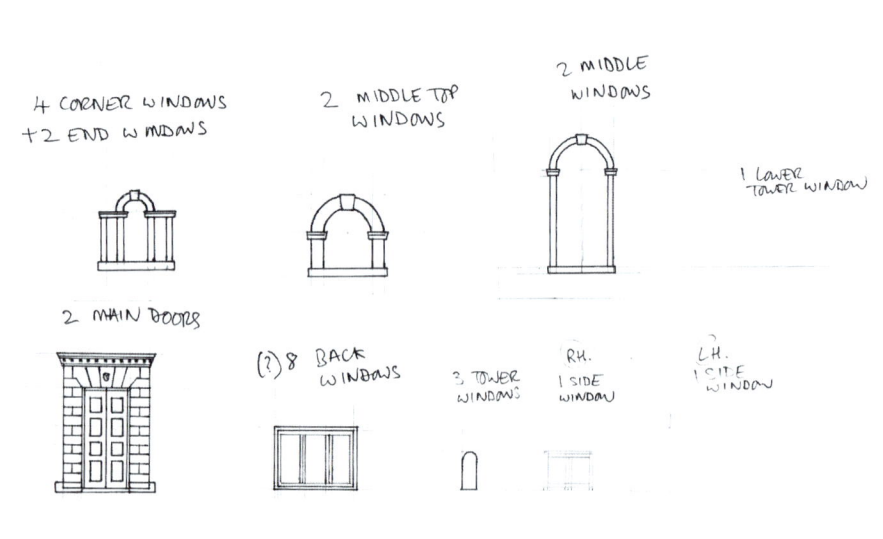

The above drawing shows all the window and door surrounds needed to make the model.

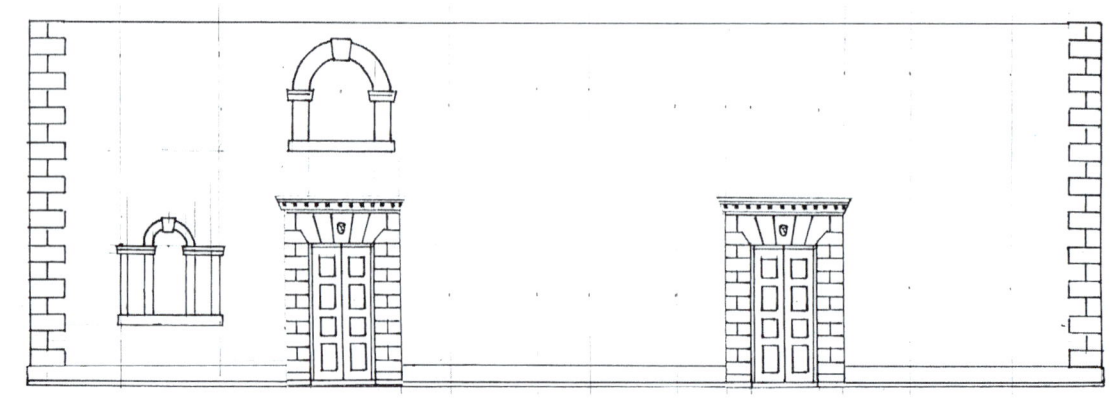

More Model Buildings - St. Mary's Church 91

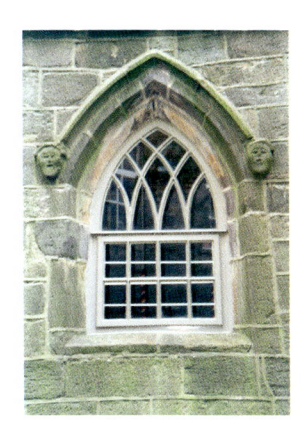

Left, is a small window near the base of the tower. The picture to the right is my model of it.

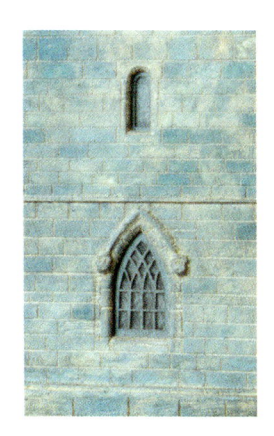

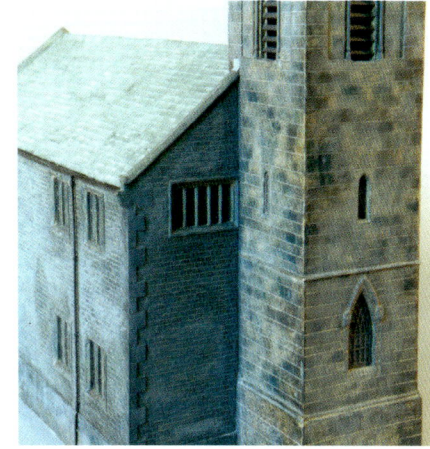

Some of these pre-digital photographs have a blue tone to them, so are not up to standard, but they are the only ones I have of the model.

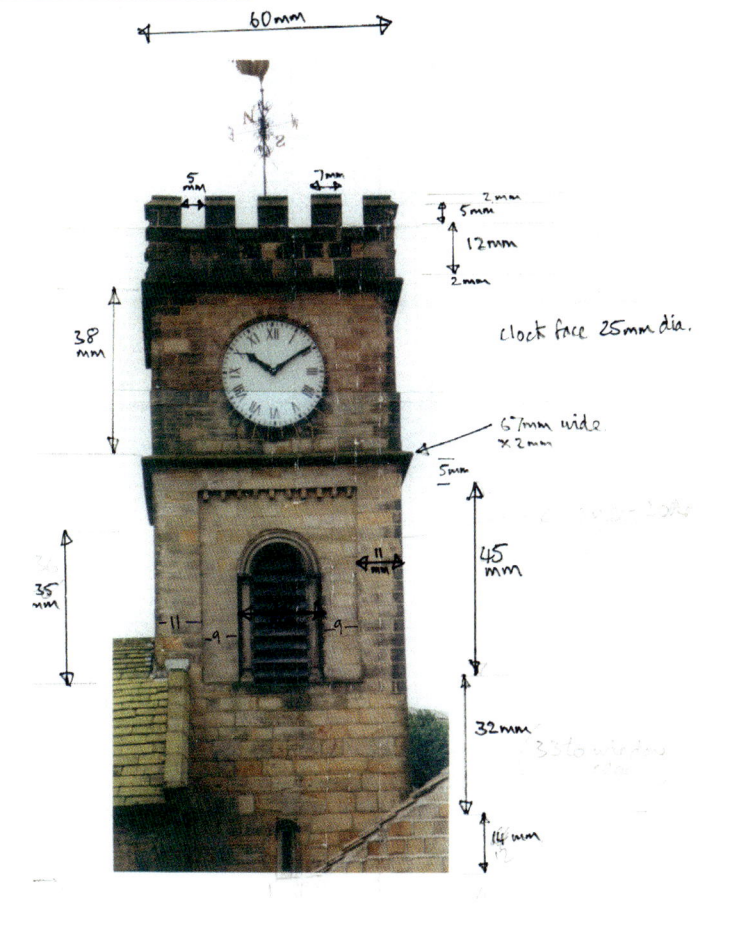

92 St. Mary's Church - *More Model Buildings*

The East wall is shown here with the rocky ground and stone steps, leading up to the back of the church.

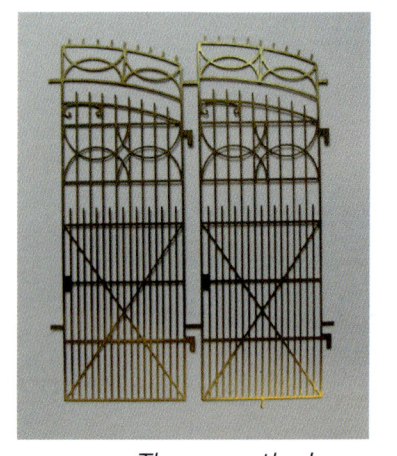

These are the brass etches that I used for the churchyard entrance, just seen in the picture to the left. I worked out the size from a photograph and drew them up on the computer.

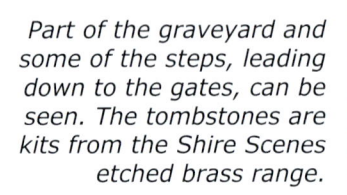

Part of the graveyard and some of the steps, leading down to the gates, can be seen. The tombstones are kits from the Shire Scenes etched brass range.

SUMMIT TUNNEL
4mm

Summit tunnel is on the Manchester to Leeds route and is located near Todmorden in West Yorkshire.

Only a small portion has been modelled inside, so that the tunnel can be as long as required on the layout.

It would have been great to have added the surrounding scenery, such as the rock cutting and the trackwork, to make a complete scene.

This model was a bit more difficult to make than originally thought. To construct the arch, I used a plastic pipe covered in Milliput and then carved the stones. Most of the remaining stones were carved from DAS modelling clay.

The real Summit Tunnel.

LOUTH STATION
4mm

This complex and decorative model was, as it looks, quite complicated in the making. It did however, look really good when it was finished and I was very pleased with the end result.

I was given scale plans, but a few minor alterations had to be made with the sizing.

Each part of the building was constructed as separate parts and the pictures here show that well. The portico in particular makes this model different. Some interior detail was requested including lighting, which in itself created a lot more work.

The wall, to the platform side, has been made and the front of the building is taking shape. Note the window recesses. This allows the etched-brass window frames to be fitted to the correct depth.

This is the right hand front gable part of the model. You can see it has been made as one unit. Note the corner stones. These are two layers of plastic, scored and bent at right angles and then attached to the wall. The ornate wall top outlines were drawn and cut out with the wall. The base plinth stops short to allow for the attached building to butt up against the wall.

The portico is now ready for the ornate stonework, seen in the top picture, to be added. That was made with brass etches, sandwiched together to get a good thickness.

More Model Buildings - Louth Station   95

The front of the model showing the entrance doorway into the booking office. The plain white plastic on the wall and the paving is where the portico will be placed. The paving actually slopes down to the left hand side, so spacers were glued underneath in the centre of the model.

Two units fixed together. The colouring of the brick walls is only different coloured plastic bricks. Everything will look the same when painted.

Here I have a book on Louth station open, so that I can see what the finished model should look like. This is the platform side.

Louth station is featured in my other book, Creating Model Buildings, but doesn't show any of the construction pictures.

Inside the booking office, showing the planked wood floor and the nice dark wood panelling for the ticket office wall. If lights are to be fitted, then quite a bit of detail will have to be added.

Platform side with the bay window of the waiting room. The step will just about disappear when the platform is in place.

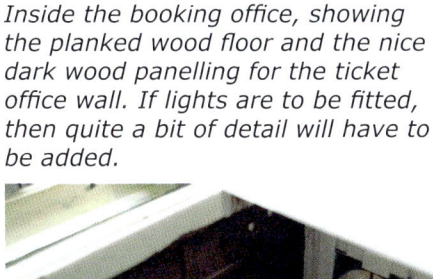

LAYOUT FOCUS -
BARMOUTH JUNCTION

4mm scale
British Railways period, 1948 - 1965

This is my own layout that I am building and is not an exhibition layout. It is permanently fixed in place, so not too many people will see it. It is not finished yet and in some of the pictures, you will notice things that need more detail on them, such as the station building. A lot more work is required to make it look really good.

It is modelled on the actual station of Barmouth Junction, later called Morfa Mawddach in the early 1960's, which is on the Welsh coast and I've tried to capture the feel of the real one as it was in steam days. Due to the usual lack of space, I have had to change things slightly to get all the tracks to go off scene and round the room.

As well as the Junction station, I am also constructing Penmaenpool station and Dolgelley goods yard. I would have liked to model the whole of Dolgelley, as it was a lovely station, but space only permitted me to do the goods yard. As I already had two stations planned, then the choice I made was the best one.

For the first two years, I was modelling it on my own, but since then, some of my friends have been helping me with its construction. I have built all the baseboards and laid all the track, but this is

This is the only entrance by road and foot and is accessed by a small lane, about half a mile from a road. The coach on the right in the bay platform will eventually be one or two camping coaches. The station building still has its roof to be modelled and is still in mock-up card.

More Model Buildings - Barmouth Junction

where my friend John Bailey came in and he has done a lot of the electrics. The layout was always going to be DCC, so I had to put bus wires all round the track and then connect it all up. Each separate piece of track and all points had positive and negative wires, which had to be joined up to these bus wires, so it was a long job. Also, each loco has a decoder installed, so you need to know which number engine you are driving.

A few years earlier, I had drawn up scale plans of the whole layout to see if it all fitted. These plans were later drawn up on lining paper, to the full size, before commencing the project.

I wanted the trains to leave a station and actually travel some distance, before entering the next station or scenic section. This meant different levels and tracks that went over or under one another to get to their destination. It made the layout quite complex in the making, but now I think it was well worth it, as it is great to operate.

For the first time, I have working signals on the layout and I have my friend Tony Geary to thank. He has made the signals and also got my loco's to work better, amongst other things. Also a first, is having a kit-built loco made for me. It is a Dukedog and made by my friend, Jonathan Matthews.

One of the main things that I wanted on the layout, to make it look the part, was decent backscenes, so I asked an artist, Sara Heller, to paint

This row of houses is down the lane from the station. The end house has an interesting design and it makes it stand out more for my model. Still more to do on the scenery, such as a few more trees, the covering up of the hinge and tidying up the ground to the left.

**This is my first layout that has been modelled on a real location, that hasn't had anything else added to it. It is also the first layout I have modelled in BR days.
With the operating sequence I've devised, it is proving to be interesting to operate as well.**

Typical Great Western signal box at the junction. The coast line is to the bottom and branch line to the top.

them for me. This has really transformed the look of the layout and given it depth. It has been painted on acrylic roll canvas, so there are no joins in the length. There is one actually, but it is on the curved part at the junction loop end, so cannot be seen.

I have made all the scenic landscaping and, of course, the buildings. You may have noticed that their aren't many of those and that is for a reason. If I had chosen an urban setting with lots of buildings, then perhaps that layout would never have been finished. As making buildings is my main job, I wouldn't have the time to make a lot of buildings for my own layout.

A sequence for operating trains has been written, which gives added interest. It takes a considerable time to get through the whole sequence, so that has made operating even more enjoyable.

Two platelayers houses stand very close to the railway track, which is between it and the rocks behind. This is taken from an actual building and is really needed to hide the railway line going through the backscene to the right.

Close-up of the houses, showing the slated side walls.

This is Gwynnant bridge and is modelled on the real one on the branch line, near Penmaenpool. It is just a tributory river that flows into the main river, which is just out of sight to the left. The actual bridge is still standing, so it was easy to measure up and take pictures to make an accurate model.

More Model Buildings - Barmouth Junction

A Manor is approaching Barmouth Junction station and will arrive in the coast line platform.

As I didn't have space for the long Barmouth bridge, I had to compromise here. The tracks actually go through the backscene on the near side of the water. The backscene was painted as an estuary, without the bridge in the scene.

The train has just come across Barmouth bridge (off-scene) and is just about to enter Barmouth Junction station. The backscene shows up well here and you can almost hear the seagulls and smell the salty sea air.

100 Barmouth Junction - *More Model Buildings*

Approaching Gwynant bridge. This is a long scenic section, about fifteen feet long by a foot wide.

The platform ends of the coast line. Just visible, are wagons on the loop line siding.

This is the road bridge, which spans both the railway and the river at Dolgelley. It is also a very convenient scenic break to go to Ruabon storage sidings. Just visible in the picture, are the ends of Dolgelley station platforms.

**This is an on-going project, so more work is gradually being done to improve and add more details.
One of the next projects will be the station of Penmaenpool, which has a good variety of buildings. The track is on an embankment, with part of the river below, so it should make a nice scenic section.**

The railway follows the river all the way along this scene at Dolgelley goods yard. The river has been made with countless layers of varnish and a small amount of acrylic paint between some of the layers. The loading dock needs finishing and also the goods shed.

More Model Buildings - Barmouth Junction 101

The nearside track is the single line from Barmouth, over the bridge. The other track is a small siding.

Some of the pictures of Barmouth Junction have been taken by Tony Geary

A view from the back of the station, looking down the lane. A loading dock can be seen on the left.

Barmouth Junction panel. The artwork for this was drawn on the computer and then I had it printed on a thin metal sheet, which has a protective coating. The holes are ready for the directional LED's. A lever-frame is being made to operate the signals and points.

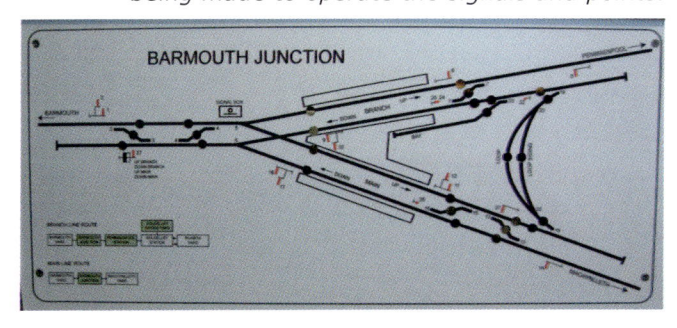

The coast line platforms, looking down towards Machynlleth.

The branch line waiting room still needs bedding in. Note the wooden platform walls. There is a mixture of wood, stone and concrete, which has been used for these platform walls. Also, the surfaces have been constructed, simulating paving, asphalt and wood.

CONSTRUCTION OF BARMOUTH JUNCTION

Having described my layout, here are pictures and an explanation of the way it was constructed.

It is quite a complex project, even though Barmouth Junction station is not very large. The way in which the trains travel to each of the scenic sections is a little complicated and takes some time to achieve. This makes my layout really interesting, as the trains actually go on a journey towards their destination.

There are three storage yards, which all take up valuable space in the room, but are really essential for operating. Barmouth Junction is on the coast and there is a line north to Pwllheli, passing through Barmouth and south to Machynlleth, where it joins the line from Aberystwyth to Shrewsbury. Also, there is a branch line that goes in-land to Ruabon, passing through Penmaenpool and Dolgelley, until it joins the main line from Shrewsbury to Chester. Therefore, I have chosen to call the storage yards the destination names of Barmouth, Machynlleth and Ruabon.

Lots of planning was needed to enable me to construct the baseboards, as there is a foot difference between the top and bottom boards. I've set the top boards to a height of four feet, which gives a good operating level.

If I'm designing and constructing layouts for clients, where possible, I usually make the backscenes curved, which gets rid of sharp square corners. This makes viewing of the layout much more

The start of the framing.

These pictures show the complex arrangement of levels. It took some time to get the desired result without having the inclines too steep. Lots of markings out, in black felt tip for the tracks, can be seen and also datum levels on each track.

More Model Buildings - Construction of Barmouth Junction

pleasing to the eye. So on Barmouth Junction, I made them all curved.

I tried to make the baseboard framing so that when the points were laid, they wouldn't be in the way of the motors, but I admit that on some of them, I got it wrong! This caused some extra work later, because some motors had to be located in an area that had no framework. Obviously, for some of them, due to other tracks going underneath and the lack of clearance, I had to do that anyway.

The track on the top comes off the junction and the lower one will go to Machynlleth yard.

Paper plan of the junction on top of the framework to check it fits OK.

In the foreground is the original one inch to a foot scale plan.

Barmouth yard was worked out using paper templates.

The lovely hand-built pointwork at the junction.

104 Construction of Barmouth Junction - *More Model Buildings*

The rockface is being carved out of builder's plaster. This has to be applied about 50mm thick, so that there is plenty of plaster to cut into and carve.

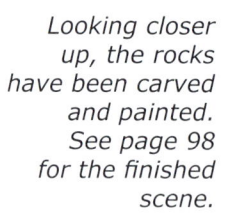

Looking closer up, the rocks have been carved and painted. See page 98 for the finished scene.

The lovely sweeping curves of Barmouth Junction trackwork.

My very temporary backscene is in place, to see how it would look. The tracks on the top are heading for the junction to the right. Pictures of the actual location can be seen, showing me what I wanted to achieve.

Another part of the temporary backscene, this time at the other end. Both coast and branch tracks are underway and the loop is being planned with paper templates.

Machynlleth storage yard and various levels that the trains have to run over, to get to their destinations.

More Model Buildings - Construction of Barmouth Junction

Barmouth Junction, showing the loop line. This was used to turn the engines round, after arriving at Barmouth, which is over the bridge. They would reverse over the bridge and go round the loop, before reversing back over the bridge, to Barmouth. The large hole in the middle will have a hinged section, so that I can get to track and stock easily.

Dolgelley goods yard track has been laid and the backscene is in place. Roads and the groundwork are taking shape, using thick card formers to get the different levels. The bare MDF in the bottom foreground will be the river. The goods shed is a card mock-up to get a feel of how it will look. Compare this picture with the one on page 100.

106 Construction of Barmouth Junction - *More Model Buildings*

Barmouth Junction waiting room. Windows and doors still have to be put in and then the roof will be constructed.

Looking towards the back of the branch waiting room. More scenery to be added at the back of the platform.

Platforms being constructed from card. Both waiting rooms have their walls well advanced, but the signal box is still a card mock-up. Note the card signals, so that I know where they will be situated.

Gwynant bridge being made.

Groundwork is advancing behind the branch platform. I've used old carpet underlay, taken the hesian backing off and then glued it in clumps to the baseboard with PVA. Colouring is done using acrylic paints, which have been well thinned.

More Model Buildings - Construction of Barmouth Junction 107

The beautiful coast-line of west wales with Barmouth bridge over the Mawddach estuary. Barmouth Junction would have been over the other side of the bridge. The railway is still in operation, but only along the coast-line, not the branch. Just one platform is used now.

Below is the view from the top of the rock outcrop. Barmouth bridge is clearly seen, with Barmouth on the other side of the esturary.

BRICK TERRACE ON HILL
4mm scale plans

This brick terrace, is situated on the steep hill, going out of town, on the Dewsbury Midland layout. Although I drew up the plans for it, it wasn't made by myself, but by Phil Taylor. It makes quite a nice contrast to the stone buildings that dominate Dewsbury.

These plans are full size, so it could be made as a project, by copying it and using the same techniques as the small terrace in my other book, Creating Model Buildings. This will give you a very different model to that one, but it could be put on the same layout quite easily.

Of course, if you wanted the road to be less steep than this, then simply adjust the alignment of the road level.

I haven't got the back elevation, but you could either place the model near to the backscene, in which case you wouldn't need to model the back wall at all, or use another model for guidance. A door and window would be needed for the ground floor and a window for the first floor. Outhouses could also be made for outside loos and coal.

The brick terrace on the Dewsbury Midland layout. This shows how steep the hill is and the necessity to make the base of the model deeper, to allow for the slope. Note also, how the ground falls away from the steps to the road. The roadway has the moving vehicles going up and down.

Looking up the hill, when the layout was being built. This shows the blue engineering brick base, which is a nice feature to the model.

More Model Buildings - Brick Terrace on Hill 109

These plans should be the correct size, but check with the measurements to make sure first.

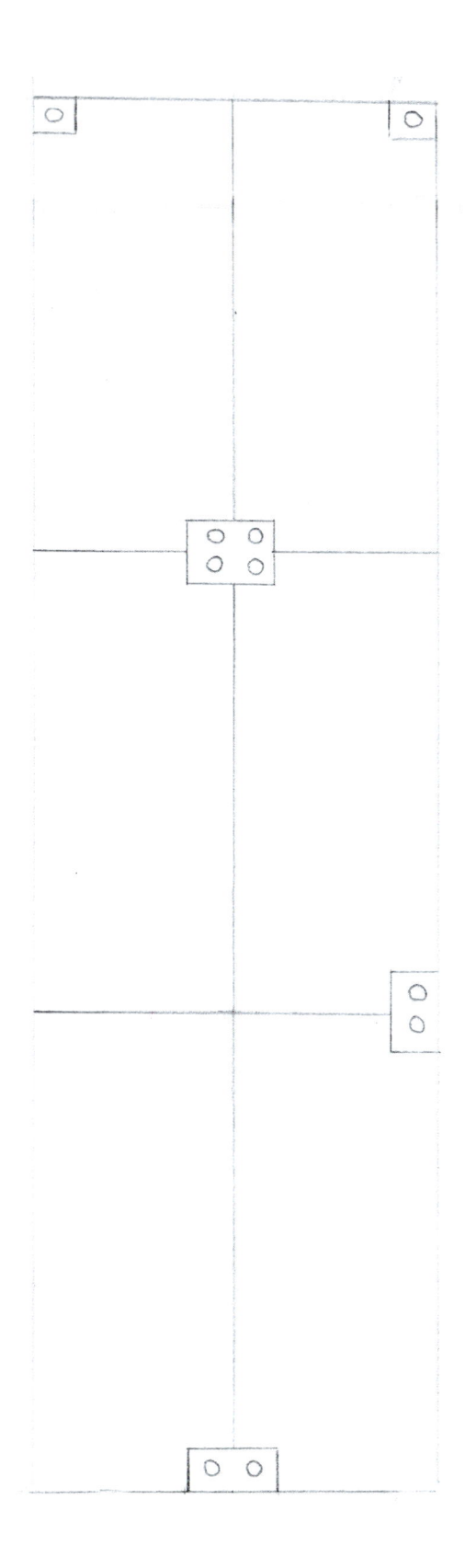

Floor plan.

SIDE
60 mm

110 Brick Terrace on Hill - *More Model Buildings*

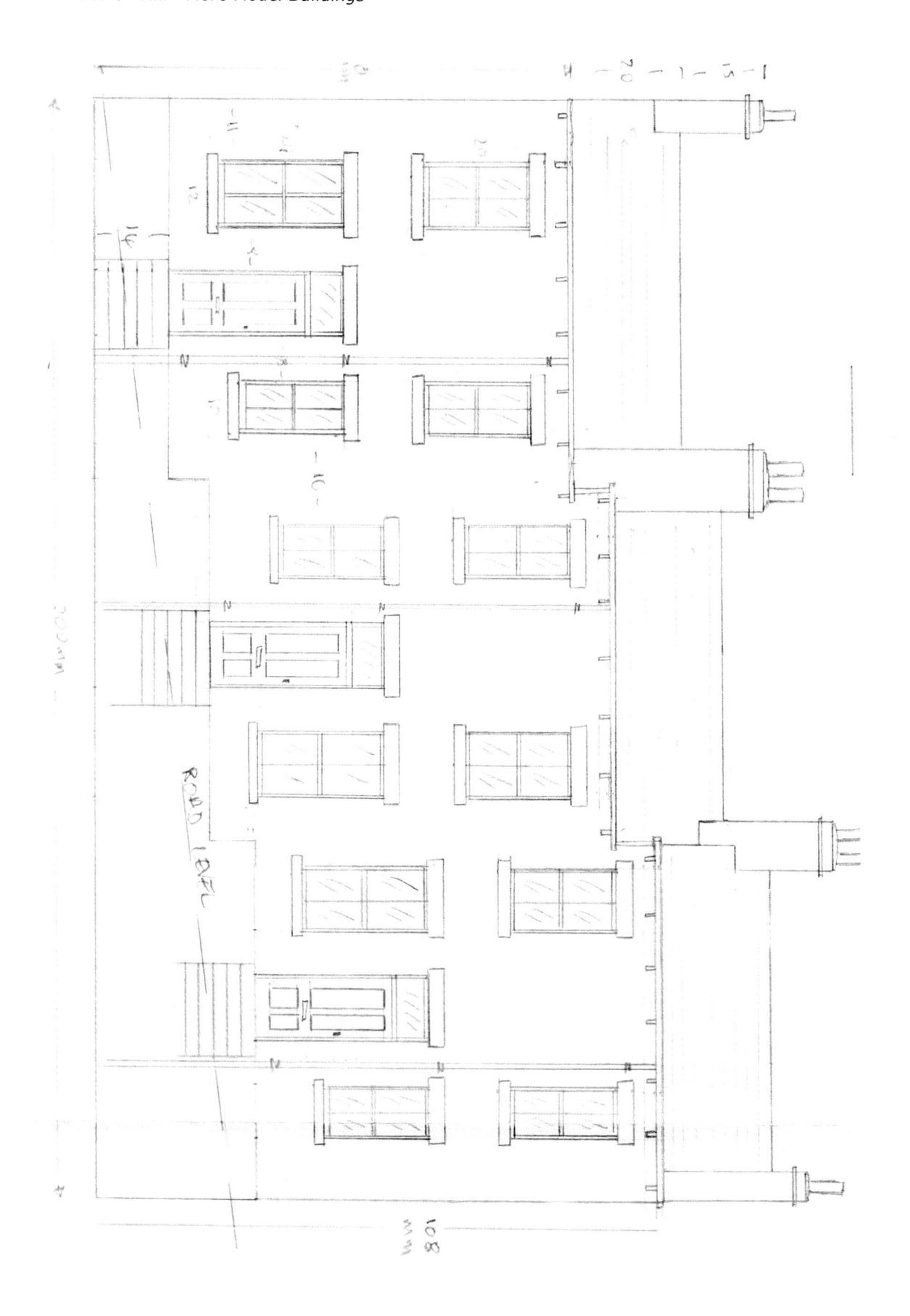

LIGHTING IN BUILDINGS

Adding lighting inside models can look really good, if done right. The big disadvantage is that all inside walls that you have constructed will have to look neat and tidy, as well as being painted. Unless the model is near to the front of the layout, then not so much detail would be needed.

Models being constructed in 4mm scale need less detailing than 7mm models, but nonetheless, all this takes time. In past models I have scribed floorboards, made panelled walls and made various bits of furniture and fireplaces, just because I had to put lights in the model.

The worst job about adding lighting is that you have to hide all the wiring, so before making a start on any model, a lot of thinking has to be done to enable the wiring to be put behind false walls etc. Also, you need to know where the wiring is going, usually through the floor somewhere, so that they can be soldered to more wiring and finally, to the switch, which will turn the lights on and off.

Another consideration, is to get access to the light itself, in case it fails in the future. This means making a detachable roof in most cases, which makes more work. I would prefer to fix the roof of a building, so you don't get any gaps between it and the walls.

Having said all this, I have seen many models which look great with lighting. The most remarkable models with lighting are the ones at Pendon Museum, which have all interior details modelled. Some of these buildings, which are on the layout, are placed quite a way from the viewer and small details cannot be seen. The Pendon models have taken a very long time to make, some a few years, but I don't have that luxury, when working to commission.

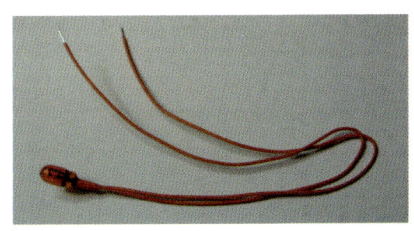

I use amber or orange grain of wheat bulbs, which come with two wires attached. This is one on the canopy and I've made a holder out of tin foil.

This is a room in the Milton Hall station and here you can see a light in the ceiling. I've made all the furniture and the fireplace and scribed the planking on the floor. This is all quite basic, but when you look through the windows, just enough detail can be seen to be convincing. When the model was completed, this viewing side was blanked out

In the waiting room below, I've put a light in each room and the wiring goes down through the central part, which is two toilets (not modelled). The tin foil just protects the plastic from the bulbs.

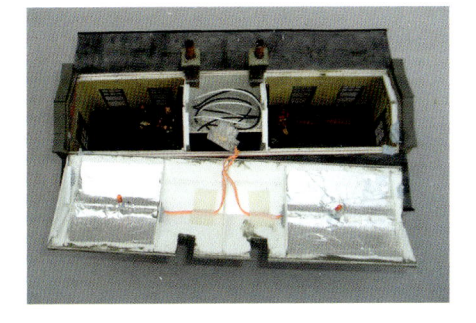

STONE TERRACE WITH END HOUSE
4mm scale plans

Here are the 4mm scale plans of a terrace, with end house. The main elevation, the side elevation and a floor plan are all included.

I've included this in the book, as a follow-up from the brick terrace on the slope, because it is a further stage in making a model. The first thing that stands out is the different roof formation. Basically, it is like two terraces together, one of them has a normal frontage, which faces the road, while the other is end on, with the entrance door on the side. This could be for another road or just a lane. Another feature of this terrace is the ornate stonework at the top of the walls. This can be done by cutting many strips of identical plastic lengths. Also on the end house is a nice ornate piece of stonework over the door, which will have to be made up from strips.

Measurements are shown and if not, they can be measured when the plans are full size. It will be easier if the two sections are made separate and then cemented together.

This might be a little bit more difficult to construct than the other terraces, but will make a good model, when completed. The finished model is on the layout Dewsbury Midland and there are two more pictures of it on page 3 of this book.

The back of the terrace is quite plain. This could be altered to suit your requirements by adding more details if needed.

More Model Buildings - Stone Terrace with End House 113

The plans are approximately half-size, so they need copying to get the correct size, or re-draw your own plan, using the measurements. The end house (plan B elevation), should be the correct size.

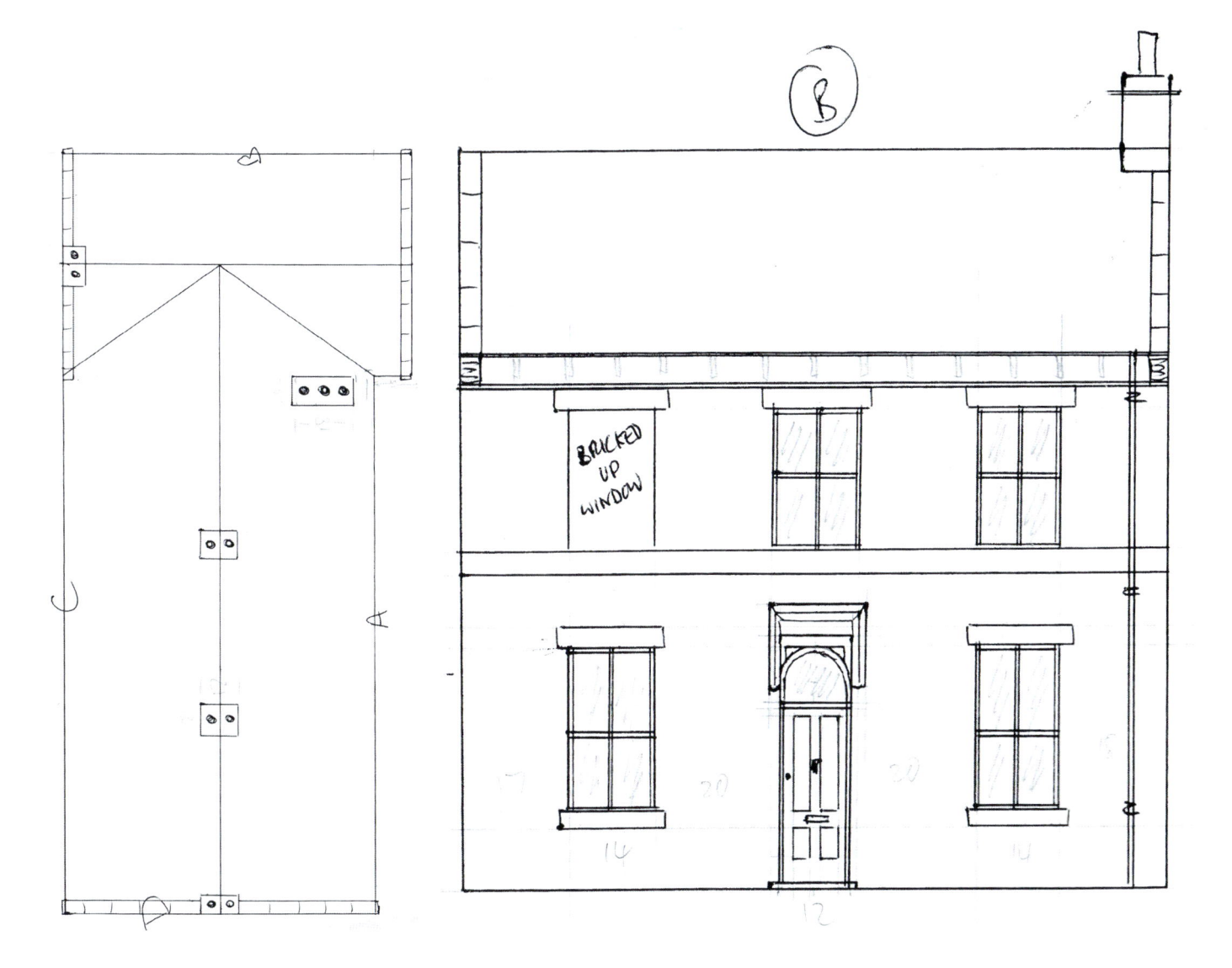

BRIDGE FOR APPLEBY
4mm

At Appleby station, on the Settle and Carlisle Railway, both platforms cross the road bridge, which is at an angle to the tracks. I followed a drawing plan and photographs, to get the correct sizing, but with the angle of the road, it wasn't going to be an easy job. The road underneath goes up hill from the front and also starts to climb at the front right hand side to get to the station yard.

As you can see from the pictures, the bridge was made on a sub-baseboard and the platforms and tracks would sit on

The finished bridge, complete with platforms and the lovely working lamps from DCC Concepts. The wires will go through the baseboard, when in position on the layout.

These other pictures show the whole of the sub-baseboard and the way in which the walls were constructed.

top of the structure. Slater's stone sheets were used for the walls, with Plastruct girders underneath for the the platforms and tracks. The main side girders are made from plastic sheet, with etched-brass rivets as overlays.

Painting was all done with Humbrol enamels and weathered using a dilute black wash and powders. The road was given two coats of paint and then weathering powders rubbed in, to give a textured surface.

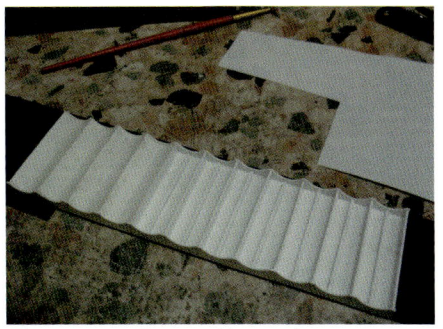

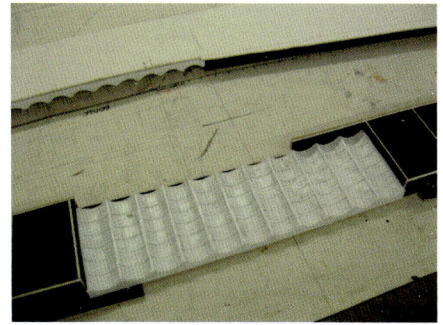

These are the sections that support the platforms. To get the curved parts, I've made the outside frame and cut the curves, using a compass cutter. Spacers and ridges were cut to size, making the sections quite strong. Thin plastic sheet was fixed in each of the sections and then strip overlays were added over the top.

The curved wall was made with plastic sheet formers first, for strength. The stone sheet was then added and kept in place with masking tape, until dry.

The painted girders are ready to be fixed in place, now the walls are glued to the base.

Information - Model Buildings

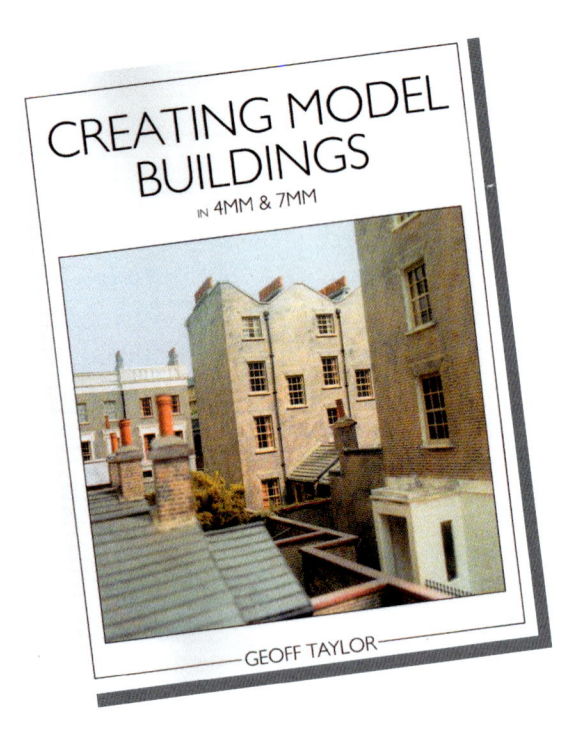

My first book on model buildings can also be purchased direct from myself.

138 pages with full colour pictures.

Construction techniques and painting of brick and stone and lots more information on building models.

For those who haven't made any buildings in plastic before, there is a full chapter on how to go about making a small terrace, from start to finish.

More details are on my website.

Visit my website for all information about my models and etches. Also, there are details about the books and DVD.

I have over 500 etches in my range at the time of going to press. A complete list of these, with pictures and prices, is on the site which is updated regularly.

I accept commission work, for both models and etches in 4mm and 7mm scales. Please contact me on the e-mail address below.

I also attend exhibitions on demo stands and on both the Gresley Beat and Dewsbury Midland layouts. See the home page of my website for exhibition dates.

Geoff Taylor (GT Buildings)

website: www.gtbuildingsmodels.co.uk

e-mail: geoffandshar@btinternet.com

Front cover picture: Fountain Hotel
Back cover picture: Louth Station